An Historical Miscellany

J. Edward Vickers MBE

The **Hallamshire** Press 1999

By the same author:

A Popular History of Sheffield
The Unseen, the Unsightly and the Amusing in Sheffield
Tales and Legends of Ancient Sheffield
From Horses to Atlanteans
The Ancient Suburbs of Sheffield
Old Sheffield—Its Streets, People and Stories
The Old and Historical Buildings of Sheffield
It's a Hard Life—An Autobiography
Saving Our Heritage

First published 1972
Reprinted 1979, 1989
This edition first published 1999

Published by The Hallamshire Press Limited
Broom Hall
Sheffield S10 2DR
England

Typeset by The Hallamshire Press Limited
Printed by Short Run Press Limited, Exeter

British Library Cataloguing in Publication Data:
A catalogue record for this book is available from the British Library.

ISBN 1 874718 44 X

CONTENTS

To my wife

Ruby

FOREWORD

by the late Professor Potter,
CBE, MA, PhD, FSA, FR, HIST S

Anyone who is interested in the continuing story of a great city will welcome this complete revision of an earlier and most attractive book from J. Edward Vickers. He has devoted many years to the study of old Sheffield, and with great skill succeeds in showing the unbroken connection between the old and the new, for he never loses sight of the interests of those now enjoying the fruit of the labours of their forefathers.

He has cast his net widely to bring into his narrative of Sheffield those outlying parts which, a century ago, were thought of as separate and are now happily integrated into what has become a metropolitan district. To this he has added a store of legends and anecdotes which will bring extra enjoyment to the many readers to whom this volume is addressed.

The Brigante Fort at Wincobank Hill. (From an oil painting by the author.)

Sheffield is Founded. (From an oil painting by the author.)

PART 1

A BRIEF HISTORY OF SHEFFIELD

Rivers always seem to make a large contribution in the early history of any great town and so it was in this locality. The main river, the Don, rises in the northern gritstone moorlands, then passes through Penistone and Stocksbridge before eventually arriving in Sheffield. On its journey it receives the Little Don, the Ewden, the Loxley and then, in the centre of Sheffield, it receives the Sheaf, which has been joined by Meers Brook and the River Porter.

In very early times, the area which we now know as Sheffield was mostly forest containing trees hundreds of years old. The hilltops were covered with bracken and heather and, on the eastern side, flat marshland and forest occupied the site of what is now the Lower Don Valley.

During the period 2400 BC to 300 BC various invaders poured into this country, but most of the settlements in this region were in the south and west and the site of Sheffield remained virgin forest. From the year 800 BC invaders came from areas of Germany and France. Known as Celts, these mixed people were mostly farmers skilled in the working of bronze and later of iron. Later, about 400 BC, came warrior bands armed with iron weapons. The Celts gradually moved northward into Yorkshire and it is probable that most of the hill-top forts were built during this time. The Celts brought with them a new language, Britonic, and it was these tribes who gave the name of Britain to this land. The tribes in this region were called Brigantes and it was they who built the fortress on Wincobank Hill.

In 55 and 54 BC the Romans invaded Britain, but these expeditions were a failure and it was almost a hundred years before the Romans came again. However, in between the two invasions by the Roman soldiers there was a peaceful Roman penetration and much of southern Britain came under the rule of Cunobelin but, after his death, his kingdom collapsed and in AD 43 the Roman Emperor, Claudius, sent another army to add Britain to their Empire.

For over four hundred years this country lay under the rule of Rome and for most of this time Britain was a well organised land. People could no longer remember the time before the Romans came—but the end was near. Reckless officers became troublemakers and the army no longer saw the defence of Britain as its main task. Raiders from the sea and land raiders from the north struck at the weakened defences. By AD 410 the Roman legions had withdrawn, leaving Britain to defend herself. Now marauders came from the north and across the North Sea.

The Angles and Saxons were barbaric Teutonic tribes who came from the region between Denmark and the mouth of the Rhine. They advanced across Britain from east to west, travelling up the rivers and along the Roman roads. They killed and enslaved the Britons and it is probable that during this time, from the middle of the fifth century to the eighth century, that the Angles made their way up the Don Valley to this area and it was these fierce, warlike people who built most of the settlements which are now combined to form the City of Sheffield.

On the banks of the River Sheaf, probably near what is now the bottom of Commercial Street, a family of Angles built a settlement of rough wooden-framed dwellings. Food was plentiful, for the River Sheaf (or Sceath, to give it its ancient spelling) was, at that time, clean and full of fish. The woods around abounded in game and so food and drink was plentiful. Eventually, the little settlement acquired a name, a field or clearing by the Sceath or Sceath Feld, now Sheffield. Around the same time many other settlements were established in the surrounding area, these becoming the suburbs of the town.

Little is known about these times until AD 829. Most of England was in the possession of Ecgbert, originally an under king of Kent, who had routed the Mercians and had been accepted as king by the East Saxons, the Anglians and all the kingdoms south of the Humber. This left only Northumbria outside his rule. The borders of Mercia and Northumbria were the River Sheaf, the Meers Brook and the Limb Brook, so Ecgbert marched to Dore with his army, but the Northumbrians submitted to him without a fight and admitted his claim to be 'King of all the English'.

Raiders from over the North Sea, fierce warriors from Scandinavia, now became an increasing threat. These Vikings penetrated up the river valleys raiding the small settlements. In AD 866 there came a large invasion of these 'Northmen' and it was around this time that they formed settlements in the Sheffield area.

The village of Dore was again important when, in AD 942, Edmund, the grandson of Alfred the Great, conquered the Danes of Mercia 'as far as where Dore divides the kingdoms of Mercia and Northumbria'. From that time onwards the Danes and the English began to live peaceably together and by the next century they were fighting side by side against their own kinsmen under King Canute.

1066—The Norman Conquest

By the time of the Norman Conquest more information becomes available of Sheffield and the surrounding district, which is named for the first time as the Manor of Hallamshire. This occurs as an entry in the Domesday Book of 1086, which

William the Conqueror ordered to be compiled so that the manors and townships of England could be assessed for value.

It is impossible in this brief history to give every detail about the Lords of Sheffield, though most of them left their mark in various ways. One of the most important to the history of Sheffield was William de Lovetot, a Norman baron from Huntingdonshire. It is probably safe to say that he was the real founder of the town of Sheffield, for he built his castle here and made it his home. The castle was built at the confluence of the Rivers Sheaf and Don in about 1150. It was of the motte and bailey type, the motte being a large mound and the bailey being an outer wall. This type of castle was constructed by digging a ditch or moat, the excavated earth being used to form a mound in the centre. If there was already a natural mound to begin with, then the earth from the ditch was used to raise it still further. Round the mound, or motte, a stout timber palisade was built and in the enclosure a wooden keep or tower would then be constructed. The keep was partly used as a dwelling house and also as dining and sleeping quarters for the garrison.

For de Lovetot's castle in Sheffield, it was unnecessary to dig a moat on two sides of the mound for, because of its location, the Rivers Sheaf and Don already formed good defences. However, to complete the moat a ditch had to be dug along the lines of what are now Waingate and Exchange Street, thereby allowing the two rivers to flow around the castle.

Because of the de Lovetots and their castle, the little town of Sheffield began to grow. So much so, that de Lovetot built a town corn mill on the side of the Don, on what today is still called Millsands. In addition to the castle and the mill, de Lovetot built a hospital called St Leonard's. This was dedicated to the relief of the sick poor and was erected outside the town on the fields at what is now Spital Hill, St Leonard's Hospital or 'Spital' giving the names to Spital Hill and Spital Fields.

The first bridge over the River Don, which got the name of 'Our Lady's Bridge' because of the adjoining small chapel dedicated to the Virgin Mary, was also constructed by de Lovetot. Also a Parish Church arose on the site of the present Anglican Cathedral.

Three generations of de Lovetots were Lords of Hallamshire covering a period of about one hundred years. It was also during this time that Robert Fitz Ranulf, Lord of Alfreton and Norton, and wealthy landowner, built Beauchief Abbey.

The de Furnivals were the next Lords of Hallamshire and it was during their time that Simon de Montfort, who was Earl of Leicester, led a rebellion against the bad rule of the King, Henry III. Because Thomas de Furnival had sided with King Henry, a party of barons, led by John de Eyvill, on their march from north Lincolnshire into Derbyshire, halted at Sheffield and proceeded to destroy the town, burning down both the wooden castle and the Parish Church. Four years later a massive stone-built castle was constructed, this lasted until the Civil War in the reign of Charles I. It was demolished in 1648 by order of Parliament after it had stood for 378 years.

Assembly Green, the Castle and Sheffield Town c. 1640. (From an oil painting by the author.)

View of Sheffield Park from the Castle c. 1580. The 6th Earl of Shrewsbury and his wife, Bess of Hardwick, converse on the battlements. (From an oil painting by the author.)

The Talbots

Sheffield's history was little affected by the first of the Talbots who spent most of their lives fighting in the King's service. However, George Talbot, who became the fourth Earl of Shrewsbury at the age of five, became one of the most prominent men in Sheffield's history.

It was he who broke the tradition of his family and decided to make Sheffield his home, living in the castle built by Lord Furnival. Having a large family and finding the castle accommodation rather cramped, he decided to build himself a country mansion which he called his Manor Lodge. This very fine building, now a ruin, had a magnificent long gallery filled with beautiful tapestries, pictures and furniture. The Lodge stood in very pleasant surroundings in a stretch of woodland which covered over 2,500 acres called Sheffield Park. Herds of deer roamed amidst the large oak and walnut trees.

Having now become a very powerful man, being Lord Steward of the King's Household and Lieutenant-General of the North, the Earl built, in Sheffield Parish Church, a chapel in which himself and his family could be buried. This came to be known as the Shrewsbury Chapel, now a very historic part of Sheffield Cathedral.

Mary, Queen of Scots

In the year 1569, Queen Elizabeth committed to the care of the Sixth Earl of Shrewsbury (another George) the most controversial woman in our history, Mary, Queen of Scots. With her assertion that she was the rightful claimant to the English throne, together with her continuous plotting against Queen Elizabeth, the latter decided that Mary should be kept in custody—the remoteness of the little town of Sheffield seemed the ideal location. Mary arrived in the town on November 28th, 1570. She was then kept for thirteen years, for some of the time in the castle, but more often in the Manor Lodge.

The legend that she was imprisoned in the turret house (or gate house) is rather far fetched as Mary had with her thirty attendants, among whom were Lord and Lady Livingstone, William Douglas, her young friend; Castel, her doctor, and Roulet, her French secretary. One of this party was left behind in Sheffield, for before Mary and her retinue left the town, Roulet died and was buried at the Parish Church.

George, Earl of Shrewsbury, got extremely tired of caring for the Scottish Queen and her party, so Queen Elizabeth allowed him to send her to Wingfield, in Derbyshire. From there Queen Mary was taken to Chartley in Staffordshire where her last plot was formed. Because of this plot she was brought to trial, condemned and, on February 8th, 1587, she was beheaded at Fotheringhay Castle.

The Seventh Earl of Shrewsbury was Gilbert, a bad-tempered person with extravagant tastes. He was the last to inherit the Lordship of Sheffield and when he

The Turret House at Manor Lodge. (Courtesy of Sheffield Libraries.)

died his property passed to his brother, Edward. However, he died after only nine months and all the Talbot estates were then divided between Gilbert's three daughters, Alethea, Mary and Elizabeth. It was through Alethea Talbot's marriage to Thomas, Earl of Arundel and Surrey, that the Talbot estates eventually came to be the property of the Dukes of Norfolk. An agent was then employed by each Duke to look after his interests in Sheffield, the Dukes themselves residing at their castle in Arundel.

How Sheffield Lost its Fine Castle

In 1606 when the Talbot estates passed to the Dukes of Norfolk, war broke out between Parliament and King Charles I. This war was fought mainly for political and religious ideals. Sheffield was now a small manufacturing town and, in religion and politics, the majority of its people, under the direction of their vicars, supported the Parliamentary side. The three leading citizens, Bright of Carbrook, Spencer of Attercliffe Hall, and Jessop of Broom Hall, were all against King Charles and keen supporters of Parliament.

Sheffield Castle had a peculiar history. Firstly, the four cannon, which made up the main defence of the castle, were taken away to Doncaster by order of the King, so that when the war broke out the Sheffield people were easily able to seize the castle and hold it for the Parliamentary side. In 1643, the King's forces marched on Rotherham, took the little town and then advanced on Sheffield. The castle was surrendered to the King's men with hardly a shot being fired.

Later, after numerous battles, the Parliamentary army retook Rotherham and when they entered Sheffield they were welcomed by the townsfolk who assisted the troops in setting up a camp on the edge of Sheffield Park. When the siege of the castle began, one Captain and a Master Gunner, in getting too close to the walls, were shot dead. Using cannons, three shots did great damage to the walls, but the troops in the castle refused to surrender. Another bombardment was therefore ordered, six more shots further breached the walls then all resistance collapsed and a parley was held to draw up terms of surrender.

The terms were most generous to the besieged and provided that, after handing over the castle, the officers of the garrison should go where they pleased, retaining horse, sword and pistol. The ordinary soldiers, providing they laid down their arms, could proceed to their homes and families and a week was allowed for the evacuation of wives, children and goods from the castle.

In 1648, under a resolution passed by the House of Commons, the castle was demolished and various parts of the building were sold to local people. Today, all that can be seen are a few remains among the foundations of the Castle Market which totally covers the site. In a room under the floor on the Castle Gate side are the remains of a wall, an arch and various pieces of stone-work and window tracery. On the Exchange Street side, under the Market floor, is part of one of the huge

The Parish Church c. 1790. (From an oil painting by the author.)

The Queen's Head Hotel in 1966. (Courtesy of Sheffield Libraries.)

round gatehouse towers and a section of the drawbridge pier. A few small relics found during excavations of the castle can also be seen in the City Museum at Weston Park.

The Growth of Sheffield Town

As the years passed, through the Lordships of the de Lovetots, the de Furnivals and the Talbots, Sheffield expanded, but only slowly. No roads led from the town to other parts of the country, only pack-horse tracks, and it was along these rough pathways that the early merchant cutlers travelled when undertaking the dangerous journey to London to sell their wares. In fact, it was not until the later part of the 18th century that Sheffield and the surrounding area acquired any reasonable roads.

The living and working conditions of the ordinary people, though poor under the feudal lords, gradually grew worse during the 18th and 19th centuries. From being almost a country village, Sheffield developed into a grimy town with tumble-down houses and poky little workshops. Sanitation was practically non-existent and disease became rampant. The once timber-framed town houses, which had already had their thatched roofs removed and replaced by heavy stone tiling, gradually deteriorated and were demolished. Today only one timbered building is left standing in the town, the Queen's Head Hotel, which was originally 'The Hall in the Pondes'. This fine house, belonging to the Castle, has now been over-renovated and the appearance spoiled.

At the beginning of the 18th century the town consisted of thirty-five streets, lanes and passages. The drainage was exceedingly primitive. Open sewers ran down the middle of the streets and into these ditches all household refuse and slops were thrown. The water from Barker's Pool, which had been constructed in 1434, was released once a month to swill these open sewers, all the filth being washed down into the River Don.

In 1794 came war with France. Sheffield lost much of its foreign trade, leaving only Germany willing to take the town's goods. Even this market dried up in 1799 and the Sheffield people were in a sorry state. Out of a population of 31,314, over ten thousand folk were in need of help. The end of the French war, in 1815, still saw terrible poverty in the town, even though a certain amount of trade had been commenced with the United States of America. This trade virtually ceased in 1830 and in 1842 the distress in the town rose to a peak unequalled. Meanwhile, to make matters worse, a cholera epidemic had struck the town in 1832, taking the lives of 402 people including the Master Cutler.

The population in 1841 had grown to nearly 111,000, and, though there were enough houses for the people, sanitation was so bad, just a communal midden in the backyard, that diseases of all kinds were commonplace. At this time the average age at which Sheffield people died was twenty-four!

Sheffield Becomes a Borough

In 1843 Sheffield was incorporated as a Borough and gradually, but very slowly, conditions improved. Hospitals, schools, colleges, churches and parks were opened and, in 1893, Sheffield was made a City. Though thousands of back-to-back, poor-class houses remained, pleasant suburbs were being developed and the stately areas of Nether Edge, Broomhall, Broomhill, Ranmoor and Fulwood were growing up the wooded hillsides. In the centre of the town a new street-building scheme was taking place and in 1875, Pinstone Street, Surrey Street and Leopold Street were pushed through the maze of little shops, works and stables. In 1895 High Street was widened and improvements made to Fitzalan Square and Angel Street. The year 1900 saw the great expansion of Sheffield begin. Norton, Woodseats, Owlerton, part of Wadsley, Hillsborough, part of Wincobank and a considerable portion of Ecclesfield, all became part of the growing city. By 1911 Sheffield had become the largest city in Yorkshire, with a population of 455,817.

St Paul's Church c. 1860. (From an oil painting by the author.)

IMPORTANT AND INTERESTING DATES IN SHEFFIELD'S HISTORY 1800–1999

1807 Establishment of first Insurance Fire Brigades.
1810 Old Town Hall opened at corner of Castle Street and Waingate—part of the building was used as a Police Court.
1811 Population 52,231.
1818 The Million Pound Act passed, enabling many churches to be built.
Sheffield Gaslight Company formed.
Regular Police Force provided for Sheffield. It consisted of a Police Surveyor, a Deputy, five Sergeants, sixteen Day Policemen and fifty-six Night Watchmen.
1819 Sheffield Canal opened.
1821 Population 65,275.
1822 Alhambra Theatre in Union Street burned down.
1823 Music Hall in Surrey Street opened.
The Sheaf Works established.
1828 Henry Clifton Sorby born in Sheffield.
1831 Population 91,692.
1832 First Sheffield Parliamentary Election—Two Members.
Present Cutlers' Hall built.
Cholera epidemic hits Sheffield.
1836 Botanical Gardens opened.
1838 Wesley College founded.
1839 Sheffield Water Company formed.
1841 Population 110,891.
1843 Sheffield incorporated as a Borough.
School of Art founded.
1844 Beginning of daily post to London.
1846 Cammells removed to Saville Street—this was the first of the East End firms.
1847 First Redmires Dam finished.
Edward Vickers made Mayor of Sheffield.

1848 The first Bench of Sheffield Magistrates appointed.
1850 The Town Post Office built in Market Place at the top end of the Shambles. (The old Meat Market.)
1851 Population 136,287.
1853 Edward Vickers erected Tapton Hall, Fulwood.
1854 Bramall Lane Cricket Ground opened and leased to the Sheffield United Cricket Club.
1855 First Cricket Match played on the new ground at Bramall Lane.
1856 The first Free Library opened.
1857 Sheffield Football Club formed—this was the world's first Football Club!
1860 John Brown, of steel works fame, built Endcliffe Hall, Fulwood, at a cost of £150,000.
1861 Population 186,178.
1864 The great Sheffield Flood.
1865 Surrey Music Hall, West Bar, burned down.
1867 Sheffield Wednesday Football Club formed.
John Brown, of Endcliffe Hall, was knighted.
The Inquiry into the Broadhead Trade Riots.
1869 The Town Council took over the Fire Services.
1870 Sheffield School Board formed.
First attempt to introduce tramways into the town.
Education Act passed. The first school to be built under this act was in Sheffield—Newhall School at Attercliffe, which opened in 1873.
1871 Population 239,941.
1873 Weston Park purchased from the Harrison family.
Broomhall, Netherthorpe and Philadelphia schools opened.
Albert Hall in Barker's Pool opened.
First tramway opened—Lady's Bridge to Attercliffe.
1874 Attercliffe, Carbrook, Crooksmoor, Lowfield, and Walkley Schools opened.
1875 The Ruskin Museum opened.
Firth Park given to the City by Mark Firth.
1876 Children's Hospital founded.
1878 Jessop Hospital for Women opened.
1879 John Tasker founded first Provincial Telephone Exchange.
Firth College opened.
1880 Central Secondary Schools in Leopold Street were founded.
1881 Population 284,508.
Winter Street Hospital founded.
1883 Town Trustees built extension to the Town Hall at the corner of Waingate and Castle Street.
1885 Sheffield returned five MPs.

1886 Meersbrook Park acquired by Sheffield Corporation.
John Tasker was first person to supply the Sheffield public with electricity.

1887 Opening of Mappin Art Gallery.
Lodge Moor Hospital founded.

1888 Water Works taken over by the Sheffield Corporation.

1889 Sheffield United Football Club was formed—to play on ground alongside of cricket pitch at Bramall Lane.

1890 Ruskin Museum removed to Meersbrook Park.

1891 Population 325,547.

1892 Hillsborough Park was developed by Sheffield Corporation.

1893 Sheffield was made a City.

1896 The Tramways acquired by the Corporation.

1897 Firth College became Sheffield University College.
The Lyceum Theatre opened.
The present Town Hall opened by Queen Victoria.
The whole of the old Town Hall at Waingate now became a Court House.

1898 The Electric Light and Power Department acquired by the City.

1899 First Electric Tramway route came into operation. It travelled between Tinsley and Nether Edge.
The Markets were bought from the Duke of Norfolk by the City.

1900 Durham Churchill & Co. was one of the first car manufacturers in Sheffield.
The Fire Station at West Bar opened.

1901 Population 401,151.

1902 Last horse-drawn tramcar ceased to run.

1904 The Central School became a Secondary School.

1905 King Edward VII opened the new buildings of the Sheffield University at Western Bank.

1906 The King Edward VII School formed by the amalgamation of the Grammar School and Wesley College.
A new Training College for teachers opened at Collegiate Crescent.
Tarmacadam for road surfacing came into use in Sheffield.

1907 *The Sports Special*, the forerunner of the *Green Un* was published. The Hippodrome was built in Cambridge Street.

1909 There were 302 miles of highways paved only with dry macadam, granite, stone, boulders or wood.
Abbeyfield Park was purchased from the Town Trust and Mr H.J. Wilson.
Millhouses Park was given to the Sheffield people by Earl Fitzwilliam.
Norfolk Park was given to the city by the Duke of Norfolk.

1910 The Head Post Office in Fitzalan Square opened. 350 postmen were employed and 636,000 letters were delivered every week.
The Palace Cinema, in Union Street, was the first purpose-built cinema in Sheffield.

1911 The Electra, in Fitzalan Square, the Phoenix, at Hillsborough, the Woodseats Picture Palace, and Heeley Electric Palace were all built during this year.
With a population of 455,817 Sheffield became the largest city in Yorkshire.
1912 Mixed bathing allowed at Glossop Road Baths for two days per week.
1914 Sheffield made a Bishopric.
The First World War began.
1916 On July lst, the Sheffield City Battalion of the York and Lancaster Regiment went into action on the Somme. Within less than one hour the battalion was virtually wiped out.
A German zeppelin got through to Sheffield. 36 bombs were dropped causing much damage and loss of life.
1918 The First World War ended.
1922 Memorial to the York and Lancaster Regiment was placed in Weston Park. It now commemorates the fallen in two World Wars.
1923 Radio, or Wireless Telegraphy, came to Sheffield. The BBC opened a local relay station called 6FL.
1925 Alderman J.G. Graves gave Graves Park to the Sheffield people for ever.
War Memorial in Barkers Pool unveiled.
1926 Sheffield Council had built 5,312 homes to rent. 1,752 being erected in this year alone.
Sheffield showed a deficit of over £30,000. Many schemes were suggested to improve this situation.
The Socialists obtained a majority on the Council. Replacing eight retiring aldermen with members of their party, they then gained complete control of Sheffield.
1929 J.G. Graves gave Concord Park to the City.
Division Street Fire Station opened.
1931 *The Sheffield Mail* was incorporated into the *Yorkshire Telegraph and Star.*
1934 Sir Oswald Mosley, the British Fascist Leader, together with several hundred of his 'Blackshirts', booked the City Hall for one evening. Surrounded by cordons of police, communists and other agitators among the crowds were prevented from attempting violence.
Central Library and Graves Art Gallery officially opened by the Duchess of York, later to become Queen Elizabeth, the Queen Mother.
1936 *HMS Sheffield,* a cruiser of the Southampton Class, was launched on July 23rd. It had a fine war record and then took part in the sinking of the German Battleships, *Bismarck,* in 1941 and the *Scharnhorst* in 1943.
1937 The Albert Hall, in Barker's Pool, burned down.
The first motor coach (charabanc) accident.
1938 The Second World War loomed on the horizon, there were many debates in the council about air-raid precautions. At one meeting a councillor

advised people not to have anything to do with them, he did not believe a hostile aeroplane could ever get as far as Sheffield!

1939 School dinners for children were a great success for many hard-pressed families and, of 57,800 children at school, 34,000 received dinners at a charge of five pence a day.

The Second World War began.

1940 On December 12th and 15th, German bombing planes raided Sheffield causing terrible destruction and loss of life. These two raids came to be known as 'the Sheffield Blitz'.

1944 A crippled United States B17 Flying Fortress crash landed in the trees of Endcliffe Park. All ten members of the crew were killed.

1945 End of the War in Europe, 8th May (V.E. Day).

Allied victory over Japan, August 15th (V.J. DAY).

1946 Whirlow Brook presented to the city by J.G. Graves Charitable Trust and the Town Trust.

From this year to 1949, in addition to the re-building of over 100 council houses bombed in 'the Blitz', over three thousand new homes were completed.

1955 The Council resumed its slum clearance programme and the old back-to-back houses were gradually demolished. The tenants were given new council houses—being built at the rate of nearly two thousand a year.

1960 Last day of tramcars in Sheffield and motor buses take over.

1961 Hallamshire Hospital opened their Out Patients Department.

1962 The Hicks Building of the University opened.

1965 Comprehensive School system adopted by Sheffield Labour Group.

1966 Opening of University Arts Tower by Queen Elizabeth, the Queen Mother. The Tower is the tallest University building in Great Britain. It stands 255 feet above ground level and has a basement floor 27 feet below court level.

1967 Two new roadways—the Greenhill and Jordanthorpe Parkways were completed and opened to traffic.

Radio Sheffield opened.

The City boundary was extended to include the village of Mosborough and surrounding area.

Castle Square (The Hole in the Road) opened.

1968 Many old streets were cleared to make way for new roads, such as Arundel Gate and Charter Row. Also Castle Square, the Furnival Gate underpass and the Charter Square subway complex were all completed.

1969 Sheffield Polytechnic founded.

1970 Sheffield changed over to North Sea Gas.

The Abbeydale Industrial Hamlet became one of the City Museums most interesting attractions.

The Hallamshire Historic Building Society was founded to protect the historic and architecturally interesting buildings of the City and its surroundings.

1971 The Crucible Theatre opened.

Jordanthorpe, Southey and Sheffield Lane Top Libraries opened.

1972 Hackenthorpe Library opened.

Telephone House in Charter Square opened. It is the largest building in the City Centre rising to 178 feet.

1973 The whole of Fargate and Norfolk Row were made into pedestrian precincts.

Extensions to the Town Hall were started.

1974 Totley Library opened.

Exchange Street was pedestrianised.

The parkway, a major link road between the city centre and the M1 Motorway was completed.

Radio Hallam opened.

1975 The Shepherd Wheel, a water-powered grinding wheel, became part of the Sheffield Museums.

Beighton Library opened.

The 50,000th house built by the Sheffield Council was completed.

1976 Bishops House at Norton Lees, after restoration, became a Museum.

1980 St Marie's Roman Catholic Church became a Cathedral.

From this year onwards, owing to trade depression, Sheffield ceased to be 'The City of Steel'.

1982 Corporal punishment in all Sheffield schools (except for Church schools, which have their own governing body) was abolished.

1983 The Octagon Centre, so called because of its shape, opened at Western Bank. The building cost £1.85 million.

1985 The Ruskin Gallery opened in Norfolk Street.

1988 Division Street Fire Station is closed. Firemen move to new H.Q. in Wellington Street.

School uniform ceased to be compulsory.

City Planning Chiefs blocked plans by developers to build a huge shopping complex in Oakes Park, Norton.

Gladstone buildings in St James Row saved from demolition after Public Enquiry.

Major plans put forward for restoration of Lyceum Theatre after it was saved from demolition by the Hallamshire Historic Buildings Society.

Plans for restoration of Canal Basin published.

Sheffield and Ecclesall Co-operative Store in Ecclesall Road is demolished.

ABC Cinema, Angel Street, is demolished.

1989 Queens Tower, Norfolk Park, for sale, price £850,00.

Royal Infirmary site becomes a Heritage Park. Norwich Union brings its headquarters to this site.
Wicker Cinema is demolished.
Hillsborough Barracks becomes a shopping mall.
The disused Division Street Fire Station sold for over £1 million.

1990 The Lyceum Theatre re-opened after restoration.
A site at Tinsley bought for Sheffield Airport.
Careless council workmen kill off many trees in Dore, Norton and Jordanthorpe, by using too-strong weed killer!
Meadow Hall Shopping Complex opened.

1991 Tudor Square, situated opposite the Lyceum and Crucible Theatres, was opened.
The Sheffield Development Corporation, working in partnership with the City Council and British Waterways started to regenerate 2,000 acres of the Lower Don Valley.
The Sheffield District Head Postmaster's area covered 630 square miles. 2,157 staff employed collecting, sorting and delivering letters and 240 administration staff. Nearly 4 million letters were posted each week in the Sheffield district.
British Telecom had 52,106 business and 102,264 residential subscribers.
Ponds Forge International Sports Centre opened by the Princess Royal.
The Graves Tennis and Leisure centre at Jordanthorpe opened by the Duchess of Kent.
The Hillsborough Leisure Complex opened.
British Rail won a National Award for its work in restoring the Wicker Arches.
The Queen and the Duke of Edinburgh opened the 12,000-seat Sheffield Arena.
Helen Sharman, Britain's first astronaut, given the Freedom of the City of Sheffield, her home city.
Ponds Forge Centre opens to the public.
World Student Games take place in Sheffield.
The bill for building facilities for the World Student Games, quoted at £147 million, rises to £212 million.
Sheffield Museums and Art Galleries suffer large financial losses.
Supertrams are planned for the city.

1992 Odeon Cinema, Arundel Gate, opens.
The first piece of track for the new Supertram is laid at Bernard Road.
Gladstone Buildings are sold for £2.4 million.
Carver Street Methodist Church is put up for sale.
Scheme to revive Canal Basin is put off for the time being.

The Queen's Head Hotel, Pond Hill, one of the oldest buildings in Sheffield, is sold to Tom Cobleigh Limited.

1993 Council wish to fill in the Castle Square Subway (known to all as 'The Hole in the Road').

Whitbreads Brewery, in Bridge Street, closed down.

Building starts on the new Crown Courts in West Bar.

Sheffield elects first Asian Lord Mayor, Coun. Qurban Hussain.

The Duke of Kent opens the Hillsborough Memorial Garden.

Restoration of the Old Queen's Head Public House.

More than 2,000 people protested against the Council's plans to sell off part of Millhouses Park.

1994 Campaign launched to save the Mappin Art Gallery from closure by the Sheffield Council.

Future of crumbling City Hall in doubt.

First part of new Supertram opens to the public. The tram to run from City Centre to Meadowhall Shopping Complex.

Mappin Art Gallery saved from closure.

Castle Square (The Hole in the Road) is filled in to make way for the Supertram route.

The Goodwin Fountain in the Town Hall Square, undergoes a facelift costing £30,000.

Mary Walton, Sheffield Librarian and historian, dies.

The fine 20-foot-high iron gates at the lower entrance to Weston Park, installed in 1875 and worth £20,000. were stolen!

Shepherd Wheel, in Whiteley Woods on the banks of the River Porter, dating back to 1584, in a ruinous state.

1995 Sheffield artist, Edward Billin, of Loxley, dies. He was a member of many art groups and has exhibited at the Royal Academy.

The Hallamshire Historic Building Society celebrated the 25th year of its inauguration. During these years it saved many of Sheffield's historic and architecturally interesting buildings.

Sheffield Forgemasters, one of the few large steelworks remaining in Sheffield, report a very successful year in spite of the recession.

Controversial proposals to convert Ecclesall Library into a public house were approved by the City Council.

The large Kelvin Flats block is demolished.

Dam House, in Crookes Valley Park, badly damaged by fire.

Canada House, the old and very fine Gas Company offices in Commercial Street, fell into serious disrepair.

Jordanthorpe Hall for sale. Price, £75,000.

Cockayne's famous store in Angel Street is demolished.

City Council face a looming debt crisis.

Council gives permission for the demolition of the old main tower at the Queen's Tower complex at Norfolk Park.

Stanley Cooper, Mace-bearer to the Lord Mayor and both universities for 16 years, dies aged 82.

City Council wants £100,000 to build new sports venues.

More cuts for Sheffield schools. Repairs under threat.

Jan Kot, architect, famous for his Town Hall extension, known as the 'Egg Box', dies aged 82.

1996 Sheffield Council complete 3,631 council homes, including the huge blocks of flats at Hyde Park and Norfolk Park. A start is made on building 127 new homes on the site of the demolished Kelvin Flats.

Sheffield has total debt of one billion pounds, that is £2,000 borrowed for every man, woman and child in the city!

One of Sheffield's famous shopping streets, The Moor, was leased for 150 years to a private company, Cordwell Property Group. Council say it will receive £1.4 million and a share in the rents.

A drought loomed over the region as water stocks reached crisis point. Most of the reservoirs only 65 per cent full.

George Cunningham, Sheffield artist, well known for his paintings of the city, dies aged 72.

Sheffield City Airport being built, cost to be around £12 million.

Stumperlow Hall, Fulwood, put up for sale.

Supertram decide to put conductors on all the trams.

Ruben Viner, one of the most influential members of the cutlery industry dies, aged 88.

Horace Dore, known to his friends by his middle name Bernard, dies aged 96. He worked for many years as manager of several cinemas, including The Wicker.

Cost of Sheffield's major sports facilities, built initially for the World Student Games, rose from £280 million to £450 million. Following refinancing of the bank loan annual repayments will peak at £30 million in 2006, instead of £50 million in 2001.

Sheffield awarded £9.5 million National Lottery Grant to build the world's first National Centre for Pop Music.

1997 The Five Weirs Walk almost completed. This walk, which also links to the Sheffield Canal Trail, will provide a footpath from the City Centre to Tinsley.

Abbeydale Industrial Hamlet is closed due to lack of money.

Historic Norton Hall put on the market.

The 15th anniversary of the sinking of *HMS Sheffield* in the Falkland Islands war was remembered at a service at Sheffield Cathedral. This warship was the second 'Sheffield' and was built in 1982.

A Public Enquiry into building a three-storey nursing home in the grounds of Broom Hall was held. The H.H.B.S. was against the application, along with others. The application was refused.

Sheffield Airport opened.

City Council decide to allow demolition of historic Shude Hill Gas Works building. An hotel is to be built on the site.

Botanical Gardens Trust hope to raise money to restore the very fine Paxton Pavilions, the Entrance Lodge and the Curator's House.

Work starts on the destruction of the flower beds and trees in the once-beautiful Peace Gardens, (formerly St Paul's Gardens).

Many bunches of flowers were laid beside the Cathedral in memory of Diana, Princess of Wales. Hundreds of people line up to enter the Cathedral to sign the book of condolence.

Many Sheffield people complain about the 'New Look' of Fargate.

Plans for a Leisure Park at the home of Sheffield United Football Club expected to be approved.

The Lord Mayor, Tony Arber, cuts a birthday cake to celebrate the centenary of the Lyceum Theatre. The Hallamshire Historic Buildings Society which saved the Lyceum from being demolished were not invited to the ceremony!

The newspapers display large pictures of sculptures intended for the Town Hall Square. As one person asked, 'Is it art or something from the scrapyard?'

1998 The Sheffield Town Trust celebrates its 700th Anniversary by selecting the most disliked sculpture, a nine-metre column in lead and gold leaf by Shirazeh Holishiary, for the centre of the Town Hall Square. The Sheffield people refuse it!

The Sheffield Cathedral is to receive a grant from English Heritage for repairs and renovation.

The Goodwin Fountain, one of Sheffield's beautiful landmarks, is demolished.

Permission is given for the historic Queen's Tower at Norfolk Park to be used as a night club.

First scheduled flight took place from Sheffield Airport.

Large department store, House of Fraser, in High Street, sold to T.J. Hughes, the Liverpool based discount chain.

Old Fire Station on Division Street opens as a plush upmarket coffee bar.

Hibbert Bros., Fine Art Dealers, at corner of Norfolk Street and Surrey Street since 1834, have to close down owing to massive rent increase by council.

Part of Millhouses Park to be transformed into a wild flower meadow.

Sheffield's Mainline buses sold to First-Group.

Old Holt House, at Abbeydale, allowed by City Council to fall into ruin. It was closed by the council shortly after a £20,000 refurbishment!

Work started on converting a large factory, Cornish Place, in the heart of industrial Sheffield, into an apartment complex.

The new look Fargate almost complete. People complain about the cobblestones hurting their feet.

The Hallamshire Hospital opens a new £1 million centre to treat people with head and neck problems.

Threat by the council to sell Norton Nurseries for housing development angers Norton residents. The nurseries are part of Graves Park which was given to the Sheffield people for ever!

New Peace Gardens are opened.

Park Hill flats are listed Grade II* much to the disgust of many people.

The old Birley Spa Bath House is set for restoration.

1999 The Lantern Tower of Sheffield Cathedral is renovated. New coloured glass panels have been fitted. The new lantern is to be dedicated by the Bishop of Sheffield.

Nether Edge to be made a Conservation Area.

Norton Free schoolchildren plant 650 trees around the school playing fields. The people of Norton raised over £200 through tree sponsorship.

The City Council approved a plan to let community groups and Heeley City Farm restore and run the Victorian Walled Garden at Meersbrook Park.

The Sheffield Graves Art Gallery has a new treasure. Sir Stanley Spencer's painting of *Zacharias and Elizabeth*, bought for £1,141,578.

Wards Brewery give £500 to the Botanical Garden's Trust.

The City Council announce that it will take at least six months before the new Peace Gardens and fountains are completely satisfactory.

The Whirlow Hall Farm Trust celebrated its 20th anniversary. Since its beginnings 400,000 children and young people have benefited from the farm.

Licensing magistrates gave their approval and granted a licence to Greenall's Brewers so that the historic Abbeydale Hall can become a £3 million public house.

St Peter's Church in Greenhill is listed as a Grade II building by English Heritage. The church was designed by Oxley and Bussey and completed in May, 1965, at a cost of £50,000.

Work on a new £4.1 million development to the Sheffield Children's Hospital was started.

The new National Centre for Popular Music was opened to the public.

Wards Brewery finally closes after attempts for a management buy-out failed.

Attercliffe Common c. 1792.

PART 2

SHEFFIELD'S ANCIENT SUBURBS

On Norwood's flowers the dew drops shine and shake;
'Up sluggards, up' and drink the morning breeze,
The birds on cloud—left Osgathorpe awake;
And Wincobank is waving all its trees
O'er subject town and farms, and villages,
And gleaming streams, and woods, and waterfalls.

Attercliffe Windmill.

Attercliffe

The name Attercliffe is derived from the village 'at the cliff'. The cliff in question being at the bend in the River Don just below where Christ Church used to stand. It is a prominent feature on mid 19th century drawings and paintings of the area.

In the Domesday Survey, Attercliffe was obviously considered more important than Sheffield in that it was mentioned first when referring to the two places, 'In Aterclive and Escafeld...'

Even up to the early 1800s Attercliffe remained a pleasant country village, in 1806 it is described as follows:

> *The immediate surroundings are those of rural beauty and its scenery of hill and dale, of wood and water, are of a most pleasing character. The clear flowing Don is well stocked with a variety of fish*[1] *and on both sides of the river are large and magnificent trees. The village is studded with plantations and orchards, and fruit trees overhang the footpath in many parts of the main street.*

Later, in 1860, Ralph Skelton, who lived in Attercliffe from 1815 to 1877, wrote:

> *There was no prettier place for miles around than Attercliffe, fine houses, Milner's, Huntsman's, Skelton's, the Vicarage, New Hall, Dr Shaw's, all finely wooded, made a picture difficult to match. Pen and pocket knife makers were busy in their little workshops, Coe and Lister, the Gasgoignes, the Millars. The shops were small and country like, the canal banks picturesque, the railway new, several farms and waving crops.*

At this period the Duke of Norfolk was the Lord of the Manor, but one of the principal landowners was the Earl Fitzwilliam. Most of the people were engaged in agriculture, pen and pocket knife manufacture and the steel trades.

The first place of worship to be built at Attercliffe was the small Chapel of Ease situated in Hilltop Cemetery. This historic chapel, built in 1629, with the aid of Stephen and John Bright of Carbrook, still stands today. After being left in a state of neglect and disrepair for many years the chapel was renovated at the time of the redevelopment of the Lower Don Valley.

In 1826 Christ Church was built as a place of worship for the rapidly expanding population. This was destroyed by enemy bombing during World War II.

The first school was the Town School built in 1779, this building subsequently being converted into almshouses. Later followed the Council schools, such as Newhall, in 1873, Attercliffe, in 1874, and Huntsman Gardens, in 1884.

Most of old Attercliffe has long since disappeared. In the 1800s one of the landmarks of the area was an old windmill with a large chimney as its neighbour. The only reminder of the windmill today is a little lane bearing its name. The chimney was demolished after it became dangerous and started swaying in high winds.

Practically all the ancient mansions are now just memories, including the Old Hall, the New Hall, and Carlton House.

The Old Lambpool Public House, Attercliffe.

Left: the house in which Sir R.A. Hadfield, world famous in the development of alloy steels, was born. Next door is the old Vestry Hall.

New Hall was a large, brick house erected by John Fell who amassed considerable wealth at the nearby iron works. His wife bequeathed the hall and estate to the Swallow family and after they ceased to live there, it was occupied by John Sanderson. When John died, the Swallows sold the estate complete to Hunt and Company who, at great expense, converted it into pleasure gardens and a sports ground.

Many folk living in Sheffield at that time would take a horse-drawn charabanc trip to Attercliffe to visit the famous Newhall Pleasure Grounds. In fact, it was considered an ideal way to spend a day's holiday!

On the estate there was a cricket ground, a racecourse, a bowling green and a maze. There were gardens with beautiful lawns, and 'lovers' walks' alongside the River Don shaded by large trees and decorated with statues. The river hereabouts was placid clear water and suitable for boating and fishing. On the east side of the grounds was a large lake, which served as a foreground to pictorial representations of fine cities. In the evenings musical concerts were given and the day's events usually finished with a large fireworks display.

There is a glimpse of the past in the name 'Salmon Pastures'. This was originally a large stretch of sandy ground alongside the Don, near Attercliffe Bridge, where salmon used to spawn.

At the time of the Sheffield Flood a cottage existed on the far end of Salmon Pastures which was occupied by an old lady named Hutchinson. How she managed to escape death during the flood was a miracle, for the cottage was shaken to its foundations by the mighty weight of water and by colliding timbers and wreckage. All around her humble abode swirled the bodies of people drowned in the flood, but luckily she managed to keep her head above water and was rescued about midday the following day.

Broughton Lane, just off Attercliffe Common, takes its name from Spence Broughton. On February 9th, 1791, Spence Broughton, once a wealthy Lincolnshire farmer, and his companion, John Oxley, held up the Sheffield and Rotherham Mail and stole the post bags. The contents of which included, amongst other letters, a bill of exchange for £123 payable to Joseph Walker of Rotherham.

Both the robbers were caught in October of the same year and were tried at York. They were both sentenced to death, but Oxley somehow managed to escape. Broughton was executed at York Tyburn on Saturday, April 3rd, 1792, and in the grey dawn of the following Monday morning his body, which had been brought back to Sheffield, was hung in chains on a gibbet near the scene of the robbery.

This event created great public interest and for the next few days the road between Sheffield and Rotherham was crowded with a moving mass of people anxious to view the wretched spectacle of the body on the gibbet. One person, horrified and broken-hearted at the sight, was the wife of Spence Broughton, who sat at an upstairs window in the nearby Arrow Inn, weeping bitterly.

Attercliffe Common, 1974.

Attercliffe—awaiting demolition.

The bones of the mail robber hung on the gibbet for thirty-six years, until they crumbled and dropped from the chains. Later, Henry Sorby of Woodbourne Hall, bought the land on which the gibbet stood and he had the post sawn down and removed to his coach house. For many years afterwards, small carved ornaments, said to be made from the gibbet post, were sold at the local public houses.

John Oxley, the escaped prisoner, also met with a gruesome end. His body was found on Loxley Moor in February, 1793, just two years after the robbery.

One of Attercliffe's most colourful and interesting characters in the late 19th and early 20th centuries, was William Law, a shoe maker.

In 1840 Mr Law opened a shop on Attercliffe Common, but moved to 743 High Street (now Attercliffe Road) in 1848. Here he made and sold many varieties of clogs, boots and shoes.

Fifteen years before his death he had a coffin made for himself and this he used to keep at the back of the shop. He made good use of the coffin by always having it full of bottles of brandy, whisky, gin, rum and elderberry wine, which he would give to all and sundry—postman, policeman or dustman.

He lived at his shop until he was 80 years old then, in 1902, he moved to one of his own houses, No. 147 Worksop Road. He owned seven houses in that road and four in Darnall Road. On the front of one of these houses he placed the following inscription:

Law bought it, Law built it,
Law gave it away.
Short was my stay
In this frail world,
All's but a seeming laughter,
Therefore mark well
Thy words and ways
For thou comes posting after.

A rather grim warning to all who passed by!
On another of his cottages was the inscription:

What faults you see in me
Strive to avoid.
Search your own hearts.
You'll be well employed.

At the east end of Attercliffe Common is CARBROOK, a name of Saxon or Celtic origin meaning a marshy or meadow stream. The Carr Brook ran behind the old Pheasant Inn in the 18th century.

Outstanding here is Carbrook Hall, the ancient home of the important Bright family. Now a public house, there still exists inside a beautiful oak-panelled parlour,

Carbrook Hall, built in 1623.

Tinsley Canal.

with a carved mantelpiece and moulded plaster ceiling, all date from 1623 when this part of the hall was built.

Tinsley

The name Tinsley is derived from the old English 'Tingas-Leah' meaning 'Field of Council'.

In the Domesday Book it is called 'Tirneslawe' and 'Tineslawe', and belonged at that time to Roger de Busli. The first Lord of Tinsley was John de Busli, Roger's father. After the de Buslis, the lordship of the manor passed to the de Tinsleys and from them to the de Wentworths, ancestors of the Fitzwilliam family.

The immense woods which then formed a part of Tinsley Park seem to have been, in Norman times, the refuge of a band of outlaws. One record tells of 'Roger de Presteman, an outlaw of Tyneslawe'.

In 1455 there was a grant by which 'Richard Wood, bailiff of Sheffield and William Swyft, of Tinsley, gave to John Hyne, of Sheffield, half a toft, built upon, and lying near Water Lane'. This William Swyft belonged to the family from which sprang Dean Jonathan Swift, the famous author of *Gulliver's Travels*.

In 1732 the River Don was made navigable to a point just below Tinsley and from there a good turn-pike road was constructed right through to Lady's Bridge, Sheffield. In course of time, the river from Tinsley was connected to Sheffield by a canal. This was opened for traffic in 1819.

The opening ceremony gave the people of Sheffield, Attercliffe and Tinsley, a gala day. All the great men of the town travelled to Tinsley to join the fleet which was to enter Sheffield. There were eleven vessels altogether, the leading boat, *Industry*, was equipped with a band, guns, flags and bunting.

When the fleet arrived at the Sheffield Docks, the event provided an excuse for unbridled feasting and speech making. There were dinners in all the taverns of the town, the principal one being at the Tontine Inn,[2] where the Earls of Surrey and Fitzwilliam led the gentry in a feast lasting for several hours.

The fact that boats could now travel right into the centre of Sheffield gave rise to a common saying which was used by mothers to reply to their children who had asked for gifts, 'Why lad (or lass)' they would say, 'you mun stop till mor ship lands at t'bottom o' Park hill an' then ar'l gi' it thee!'[3]

In 1750, a small school was erected in Tinsley, chiefly supported by money from Earl Fitzwilliam. Then, in 1798, there was considerable excitement in the village when a man named Hollingworth, together with a friend, broke into a shoe-maker's shop and stole a quantity of leather and hides. In a struggle with the owner, Hollingworth lost his hat and in his haste to escape he picked up a hat belonging to the shoemaker. Later, police managed to trace Hollingworth, and through him his companion, because of the hatter's name on the band inside the hat he had left behind in the shop. At their subsequent trial both men were sentenced to death and hanged![4]

In the late 18th century and throughout the 19th century, industry gradually took over the area. Tinsley lost all its pleasant rural aspects, eventually becoming known just for its collieries, iron, steel, and wire works.

Tinsley Park Cemetery.

Darnall

Formerly a small village on the Worksop road, the name Darnall derives from 'Derne Halh', meaning a secluded nook of land. Darnall was not mentioned in the Domesday survey and although there existed a family called de Darnall, their name is not mentioned in a list of the gentry of Henry III's reign. However, in 1641, William Spencer of Attercliffe Hall acquired the manor and this descended entire to his lineal heir, William Spencer of Bramley Grange.

In the 1860s Darnall was inhabited mainly by farmers and persons employed in the coal mines. The principal owners of this small manor were now the Chappell and Staniforth families.

The Staniforths built a hall in the centre of the village in 1723, this has long since been demolished. After the Staniforths, the house became the residence of Henry Howard, the father of the Duke of Norfolk. Later, in 1845, the hall was turned into a private lunatic asylum, but afterwards, became a private residence again.

Handsworth Church.

Bramley Hall, Handsworth, built in the 18th century.

Horse trough at Handsworth, 1978.

Cross Keys Inn, Handsworth, 1974.

One of Darnall's sons was William Walker, who died here in the year 1700. Walker is reputed to be the executioner of King Charles I.

In the records of York Castle for the year 1775, is the entry:

> *John Vickers, of Attercliffe, who was charged with robbing John Staniforth, of Darnall, of 3/6d, a sack containing horn for knife scales, a leg of mutton, 6 lb of sugar, and some flax. For this and for stealing from John Murfin, 3½d in copper, a bad shilling, a breast of mutton and ½lb of butter, he was hanged this same year.*

The Church of the Holy Trinity was built in 1840 and in 1855 a small hospital was rebuilt by the Staniforth family, who allowed the inmates 21/- (£1.05) yearly, together with a supply of coal. The first council school, in Darnall Road, was opened in 1875.

Just outside the village stood Captain Jeffcock's fine country house, High Hazels. Nearby was an ancient cricket ground belonging to Mr Vickers, here many great matches were played.

Many of the colliers of the village kept greyhounds and in 1874 one of these colliers took his dog, which he valued at £40, to the veterinary surgeon. The miner told the vet that the greyhound 'was not reight' and would not eat her food. On being asked on what he fed the dog, he was told that each week she was given two nice legs of Welsh mutton and in between, fresh eggs and wine, sometimes sherry and sometimes port! The collier earned about 50/- (£2.50) a week, his wife and children had to be content with scraps so that the greyhound might be well fed.

Handsworth

The derivation of the name of Handsworth is 'Hand's Worth', meaning the enclosure round a homestead belonging to Hand. The village is mentioned in the Domesday Book as 'Handeswrde', the value at that time being 40/- (£2.00).

Before the Norman Conquest, a lord of Danish descent, called Torchil, held the manor. Later Handsworth, with many other vast tracts of land, was given by William the Conqueror to his half brother, Robert, Count of Mortain. As with so much of the land in this area, the district came eventually into the possession of the de Lovetots.

It was probably William de Lovetot who built the first Church of St Mary in the middle of the 12th century. The Church House, now the Cross Keys Inn, was used by the chaplains and lay-clerks and was built about 1250. In this area there was formerly a mansion belonging to the Earls of Shrewsbury and tradition says Mary, Queen of Scots, may have stayed at this house for a short period during her imprisonment in Sheffield.

According to the census of 1811, Handsworth Parish, which covered a large area and contained villages such as Woodhouse Mill and Richmond, then contained

308 houses and 1,424 inhabitants who were chiefly employed in agriculture, cutlery and collieries.

Among the old buildings still standing in Handsworth the finest is Bramley Hall, a beautiful Georgian house, kept in perfect condition by the present owner. The name of the district, Bramley, comes from the old English 'Braemel-Leah' meaning the clearing overgrown with brambles.

Nearby is Cinderhill, an old English name meaning 'the dross hill'. Here was situated a Quaker colony said to number several thousand in 1654.

There is an old story of George Fox, the Quaker leader, who was being hunted by soldiers who wished to arrest him. A friend warned Fox that the soldiers were approaching Cinderhill and, knowing that escape by running away was impossible, Fox walked down the hill to the soldiers and calmly asked the Captain of the Dragoons for whom they were looking. On being told 'George Fox, the leader of the Quakers' he directed the men to a spot behind the house where he said he had seen Fox a short time before. Then while the soldiers were searching in that area, the Quaker leader made his escape.

At the nearby once pretty village of WOODHOUSE, derived from the Old English 'Wodehus' meaning a house in a wood, most of the old cottages and farms have been demolished to make way for a housing estate. The oldest cottage, built in the 15th century, was at 25 Market Square. Originally a timber-framed house interleaved with wattle and daub, it was stone faced in 1656. Preserved in Woodhouse are, the Cross Daggers a two-storey stone-built house of 1658, the base of the Market Cross and the old village stocks, all now in the midst of modern development.

To the south west of Handsworth was the pleasant village of RICHMOND. Here amidst the little cottages was a farmstead, Richmond Hall Farm, built in 1668. It was owned for a time by Burrows Trippett, who died in 1772 and was buried in Handsworth churchyard. The farm was demolished, along with most of the cottages, in 1966, but ancient gateposts still stand, looking rather incongruous, in front of the modern buildings that have taken the place of the farmhouse. These gateposts are believed to have once stood at the top entrance to the vast Sheffield Park.[5]

Brightside

Brightside means 'Brik's ploughed land' and is a very ancient village. In the time of Henry VI the name was written as Brekesherth, for in a deed of that time Thomas de Furnival gave to the monks of Worksop five marks yearly 'from his mills at Brekesherth'. Also at this date, John Brekesherd was a plaintiff respecting lands in Sheffield, Kimberworth, Tinsley and Brinsford (Brincliffe). In another deed during the reign of Elizabeth I, Brightside was written as Brixard.

The Brightside Byerlow, which included Brightside, Pitsmoor and Crabtree, had just 822 houses in 1796, and a population of 2,186. However, most of the people lived quite near to Sheffield in the Wicker and Bridgehouses area.

The Duke of Norfolk was Lord of the Manor and, in 1860, Brightside was recorded as being:

> *A considerable village, pleasantly situated on the banks of the Don, about 2¼ miles E.N.E. of Sheffield. The manufacture of steel, forks, etc., are the principal trades carried on here.*

The Church of St Thomas was opened in 1854 on the site of land given by the Earl Fitzwilliam, and a small school was built midway between Grimesthorpe and Brightside in 1802. The school held a total of 65 children and was built on land given by the Duke of Norfolk. Later, in 1880, Brightside Council School was opened.

Grimesthorpe

The name of Grimesthorpe comes from the old Norse and signifies 'Grim's outlying farmstead'. In Saxon times this was the manor of Grimshaw, and Ulfac was the last Saxon owner. The manor afterwards passed to de Busli, then to the de Lovetots and in course of time it came into the possession of the Dukes of Norfolk.

Probably Grimesthorpe's most noted family was the Saundersons whose ancestors were Peers of England and Ireland, and was the family from which came Robert Saunderson, Bishop of Lincoln in 1660.

In 1870 the now rather dilapidated Grimesthorpe Road was an extremely pleasant country lane and there were many lovely walks in the large surrounding woods. The last of the ancient cottages of Grimesthorpe were demolished some years ago, leaving only an old iron pump as a reminder of the time when, as Hunter tells us '...the village was pleasantly situated on the sloping side of Wincobank Hill, and close beneath the wood with which all the higher parts of that eminence was covered'. This iron pump was erected in the 19th century to replace a much earlier wooden one.

On the summit of Wincobank Hill can still be seen the remains of the camp, or fort, constructed by the Brigantes, the British tribes who had settled in western and southern Yorkshire. The camp was elliptical in form, with its vellum and ditch enclosing an area of several acres. Within its bounds the Brigantes clustered together in huts when the enemy threatened, but during times of comparative security they would dwell on the slopes of the hill outside.

It is probable that here at Wincobank the Brigantes attempted to defend their land from the advancing Romans who came from the large fort they had built at Templeborough in AD 54.

In ancient times the scenery around Wincobank was very beautiful, with huge trees covering the slopes of the hill. John Nixon, of Wincobank, wrote a poem in the 1800s entitled *Wincobank Hill* and though not great poetry, his verses do give us an idea of how this area must have appeared.

Old cottages being demolished at Grimesthorpe.

Pitsmoor Toll Bar in 1870. It was built in 1836.

On Nature's vast grandeurs we look with delight,
The scene all around is a beautiful sight,
The flowers with fragrance the air they do fill,
These are the productions of Wincobank Hill.
How lovely, delightful, transporting it looks,
All around we see forests and meadows and brooks,
Where sweet purling waters down the valleys do rill,
These are the beauties of Wincobank Hill.

Though all the trees were cut down, the Pitsmoor side of the hill is now beginning to be covered with young trees again. The south-east side is, however, now almost entirely built over with modern houses and a large rubbish tip covers the remainder.

To the west of Wincobank lies SHIRECLIFFE, a very fitting name, coming as it does from 'Scir-cliff' meaning 'a bright, steep hillside'.

Shirecliffe or 'Shiercliffe', was the ancient estate of the de Mounteney family, descendants of Sir Robert de Mounteney, grandson of Maud de Lovetot, in the time of Henry III. The seat of the de Mounteney's was Shirecliffe Hall, a fine house unfortunately demolished in the early 1800s.

Lying along the banks of the River Don, at the foot of the hill where Shirecliffe Hall stood, is NEEPSEND, a name that probably means 'the house of the water spirit'. This was once a very small country hamlet where there existed a corn mill built in 1795.

Neepsend is now completely industrialised and all the once-rural area is covered with works and factories of various trades.

Pitsmoor

Originally called 'Or-pits', after the pits from which ore was obtained. Except for these pits, the area was mostly agricultural or thick woodland.

Some of the large woods in the region of Pitsmoor—all of which in the 19th century belonged to the Duke of Norfolk, Lord of the Manor—were Wincobank Wood, Hall Carr Wood, Burnt Greave, Great Roe Wood, Shirecliffe Park and Cook Wood. In the Spring they were richly carpeted with bluebells, wild anemones and pansies. Now, however, most of these woods have, of course, disappeared.

Practically all the last vestiges of Pitsmoor village have vanished also, but it is still possible to see the old Toll Bar House, standing at the junction of the Burngreave and Pitsmoor Roads. Abbeyfield House can still be seen in the park of the same name, but the ancient cottages, called The Pass Houses, have been demolished. Here lived some of the miners who worked in Pitsmoor Pit.

The colliery was approached by Grimesthorpe Lane, a very old country road, and it was here that carts were backed under the chutes to be loaded with coal. The water pumped from the pit ran down a broad culvert on the side of the lane as far as the present Burngreave Vestry Hall. At this point it was joined by the burn (or brook) which had its rise in Old Park Wood. The water ran by Ivy Cottage in Pitsmoor Road, filled a horse trough situated in the garden wall, continued across the road, then through the glen where Burngreave Wesleyan Church was built. It then crossed the road again to run down the left hand side of Burngreave Road.

In between Pitsmoor and Firvale was the hamlet of CRABTREE, which preserved its pleasant rural aspect up until a few years ago. Now, many of the 17th- and 18th-century cottages have been demolished to make way for a modern housing estate. One pretty cottage still remains, Rose Cottage which was built over 300 years ago.

The district between FIRSHILL and FIRVALE was often known as 'Pitsmoor Firs' and this brings to mind an extract from a poem by the Sheffield poet and ballad writer, Joseph Mather.

Last Easter Sunday with bat, stick and trip,
To Pitsmoor Firs I did eagerly trip,
But soon got fast in a quick-set edge.
A Methodist preacher, good natured and stout,
Took hold of my shoulders and lifted me out,
And said, 'Young man, take advice from a stranger,
Permit me with freedom to tell thee thy danger,
Thou art on the road to Loxley Edge!'[6]

To the north of Pitsmoor were the small hamlets of Southey, Norwood and Longley.

Bridle path to Moonshine Lane, Southey.

SOUTHEY was the home of the Twybell family[7] as early as 1610. James Twybell was an important man, holding office in the Earl of Shrewsbury's household. In a survey of 1637, he is shown as 'holding at will a tenement called Southall (Southey) and lands at a yearly rent of £20'.

Up to the early 1900s Southey remained a quiet little village, but eventually the Sheffield Corporation built a large housing estate there and now not one vestige of the old Southey remains.

LONGLEY derives its name from 'Lang-Leah' meaning a long clearing. This, also, is now a large housing estate, with very few buildings left as a reminder of previous days.

Raisen Hall, a fine 17th-century building that was situated on the south side of Herries Road, was demolished many years ago. First a cinema and now a supermarket taking its place.

At SHIREGREEN, a name meaning the 'bright meadowland', there existed one of the oldest farmsteads in that area, Crowder House. This building was mentioned in deeds of 1402 when Julian Wilkinson left the house and estate to his son. In the 1800s it was converted into a modern residence by Bernard Wake of Sheffield, all the interior fittings being skilfully preserved—the fine oak-panelling, oak doors and leaded windows.

The cottages that made up most of Shiregreen were called the Bell Houses and the Hatfield Houses, hence the names, Bellhouse Road and Hatfield House lane. In the mid nineteenth century most of the inhabitants were either farm workers or fork makers.

An interesting cruck barn, probably built by Norman monks eight hundred years ago, can be seen at OAKS FOLD, a former little hamlet, at the entrance to Concord Park. The front wall of the barn, which was in danger of collapse, was rebuilt by the Sheffield Corporation some years ago. Inside the barn can be seen the wonderful old crucks and even part of the daub and wattle filling.

To the south of Shiregreen, near Firvale, lies OSGATHORPE. This is an old Norse name meaning 'Osgar's outlying farmstead'. Here was Osgathorpe Cottage, a house built on the site of a much older building. The Wake family were owners of much of the land in this area from 1750 to 1900. Most of Osgathorpe was built over in the nineteenth century.

BURNGREAVE derives its name from 'Burn', meaning a stream, and 'Greave', a grove.

Where Brunswick Road now runs, near Grimesthorpe Road, was the upper part of a lane called Tomcross Lane. This was a dark and lonesome spot overhung with tall trees and skirting the grounds of Burngreave House.

Here, in 1848, a tobacconist named Riley, who had a shop in Fargate, was murdered one night on his way home. His watch was afterwards found in a turnip field just below the Tea Garden Cottage. This house had a very pleasant garden, with leafy arbours, seats and tables. A little lane called Tea Garden Terrace still exists to remind us of this once delightful spot.

Wadsley

Wadsley got its name from the Old English 'Wadde's Leah', meaning Wadde's forest clearing.

Before the Norman Conquest, the owner was a Saxon lord called Aldene, but at the time of the Domesday Survey all his estate, like so many others in the north, was just wasteland.

The district then became the seat of the de Wadsleys, the first being Roger, who lived at the same time as Ralph, the first Lord of Ecclesall. In 1307 Robert de Wadsley was then lord, for at this time Edward I granted him 'a market, on a Friday, at his manor at Rotherham, and a fair there for three days'. During the time of Henry VI, Edmund de Wadsley held the manor, from the Earl of Shrewsbury, as the fourth part of his knight's fee.

It appears that the ancient owners of Wadsley Hall were accustomed to entertain twelve men and their horses every Christmas for twelve days and that, at their departure, each man was expected to stick a large pin or needle into the wooden mantelpiece over the fireplace.[8]

Wadsley Hall is still in existence, although it was much altered by George Bamforth in 1722. Many famous and interesting people have had possession of this historic house, including the 6th and 7th Earls of Shrewsbury, the Dukes of Norfolk, the Creswick family and Sir John Fowler, designer of the Forth Bridge. Near to Wadsley Hall was Dykes Hall, a fine house rebuilt by John Fowler in 1852.

At what is now called Wadsley Bridge was a ford across the Don for cattle and carts, with a row of stepping stones, known as the Lepping Stones, for pedestrians. The stepping stones across the River Don occupied a line about thirty yards below the Crescent Bridge, near the entrance to what is now the Wednesday Football Ground. Pedestrians wishing to cross the river found it necessary to leap from stone to stone. Later a wooden bridge was built and there are bills for repairs to this bridge dated 1716, 1748 and 1762. A stone bridge was built to replace the wooden structure in 1777.

A directory of 1862 shows a large population of Wadsley as being employed in the manufacture of pocket knives, the remainder being mostly farmers, shoemakers and tailors.

To the west of Wadsley village stands Loxley House, a fine three-storey stone building of 1826. The house was until recently used by the Sheffield Sea Cadets.

On Loxley Edge, in the year 1783, a man called Frank Fern murdered, in the course of robbery, a jeweller who was passing over the common. Fern was captured the following evening. At his trial he was found guilty and later was executed. His body

Old Longley Farm.

Wadsley Village.

Wadsley Stocks.

Wadsley Hall, built in 1722.

The Lepping Stones at Wadsley Bridge, 1770.

was then hung in chains on a gibbet fixed near the scene of his crime and it was not until Christmas Day, 1797, fourteen years later, that the skeleton fell from the chains.

As late as 1810 the gibbet post was still standing on Loxley Edge and it is said that should anyone venture over this waste at midnight, he or she will hear, above the wailing of the wind, the horrible clanking of the gibbet chains!

To the east of Wadsley lies OWLERTON, the name deriving from 'Alor-tún', meaning a farmstead by the elders.

The earliest lords of this district were the Creswicks, who lived at Owlerton Hall, a building that was converted into tenements and has now been demolished.

In the 18th century a well of 'holy water' was discovered which was said to have wonderful medicinal powers. The people of Sheffield made great haste to go to Owlerton to partake of this potent water and what they could not swallow on the spot, they carried away in cans and bottles.

It is also recorded that about this time there lived at the Burgoyne Arms, a giant of a man named Hales. He is said to have been 7 feet 8 inches in height and to have weighed over 29 stones.

Very little remains of the old Owlerton today, the last ancient and picturesque cottages in Leppings Lane being demolished during 1969 and 1970.

Malin Bridge

The name Malin probably derives from 'Melum' meaning worn stones or pebbles in the bed of the river.

This area was famous in ancient times for its water-wheels, which were numerous along the Loxley and Rivelin. One of these wheels can still be seen at the Old Corn Mill at the bottom of Stannington Road. This is an underflow wheel, which is rare compared with the more usual type that are turned by the water flooding over the top.

Malin Bridge and the surrounding area were severely affected by the Sheffield Flood. Between midnight on the Friday and one o'clock in the morning of Saturday, March 12th, 1864, the large dam at Bradfield burst its banks and, during this short period, 700,000,000 gallons of water swept down the valley destroying all that was in its path.

A local poet described the scene after this terrible event as follows:

From Bradfield Hills to Bradfield Dale,
Damflask and Malin Bridge,
And all along the green-bank side,
The gorge and o'er the Ridge;
From Loxley on to Owlerton,
Across and o'er Neepsend,
And down the valley of the Don,
In every turn and bend;
From Hillsbro' on to Harvest Lane,

And all the lowlands round,
Along the Wicker and its ways,
Where'er a path was found,
The huge, uproarious sea had worked
Its devastating track,
Engulfing all within its reach
In universal wreck.
Uprooted trees, logs, bales and beams.
Great heaps of brick and stone,
And mighty engines, ripped and cracked,
Like toys about were thrown;
A thousand beings homeless made,
Upon the damp ground stood,
Pale, shivering in the cold March wind,
Knee deep in slime and mud.

As a result of this dreadful calamity, 798 houses were destroyed, 4,357 flooded, and over 270 people were drowned.

Hillsborough

Hillsborough was given its name by Thomas Steade of Burrowlee House and Hillsborough Hall. This was done as a compliment to Lord Downshire, one of his patrons. Hillsborough Hall is situated in Hillsborough Park and was built in 1779 by the aforementioned Thomas Steade. The house was sold to the Sheffield Corporation in 1892 and is now used as a branch library.

The Barracks, usually called the New Barracks, to distinguish them from ones built in 1794 a little nearer the town, are situated between the Penistone and Langsett Roads. Built in 1850 they covered an area of 25½ acres and, at that time, it was one of the largest military depots in the country. There was accommodation for two regiments, one of cavalry and another of infantry.

The first regiment to be stationed there was the 22nd of Foot. As there was no Officers' Mess at that time, the officers used to dine at the Hillsborough Inn. It is said that the officers had a rather sadistic brand of humour in that they amused themselves by heating small coins in the fire, then throwing them to the poor children outside in the street.

Crookesmoor

The Crookes Moor was in olden times chiefly noted for its reservoirs and racecourse.

The latter stood where Fulwood Road is now and there was a large grandstand erected by the wealthier inhabitants of Sheffield. The races are first mentioned in

Mulehouse Road, Crookes, 1890.

View from Crookes, 1826.

A farm at Crookes, 1890.

1711, and in 1713 it is recorded that the Town Trustees were 'at charges to get horses to the races'. In 1781, when the land was enclosed, these were discontinued and a few years later the grandstand was taken down.

James Wills, in a poem about the Crookesmoor Races published in 1827, starts his verse by writing:

> *A noble racecourse, formed of hill and dale,*
> *Grandstand and starting post fenced round with rail...*

It is traditionally said that any person had the right to erect a dwelling house for himself and family on waste land between the setting and the rising of the sun, and that if he raised smoke (i.e. lit a fire) in that period he was irremovable.

So, in the year 1789, a man called Pinder built a house of sods and stones and other odds and ends, on waste ground at Crookesmoor. Starting just after sundown and working very quickly, he had his rough house built just before sunrise the following morning and before anyone arrived on the scene smoke was pouring from the chimney!

This house became known as 'Mushroom Hall' because it sprang up in the night, and great numbers of people journeyed from Sheffield to see the 'hall' out of curiosity.

Crookes

The derivation of the name Crookes is from the Old Norse 'Krkor', meaning a nook or corner of land. An early mention of Crookes was in an inheritance from John de Crokes to Roger Myle in 1447.

Crookes started as a very straggling settlement and as late as 1790 many of the mediaeval open field patterns still survived in a remarkable state of preservation. Some of the present roads are named after the old fields, such as Truswell Road, and Headlands Road and Drive.

The first school in the village was founded by William Ronksley of Fulwood. He gave the sum of £100:

> *to and for the use of a school to be built or purchased in or near Crookes in the Parish of Sheffield for ever, for which 12 children of the poorer sort be chosen out of Crookes aforesaid and out of the neighbourhood thereof shall be taught to read English only.*

Later, in 1794, a larger school was erected by the local inhabitants.

In the nineteenth century Crookes was regarded as one of the holiday spots of Sheffield, healthy and invigorating! Thomas Asline Ward, writing to a friend in 1855, said, 'I find that your son has taken a partner and gone to Crookes for the country air. I am sorry his wife requires it and hope her health will soon be restored'.

A rather amusing incident occurred at Crookes in 1870, when the Prince and Princess of Wales came to Sheffield to open Firth Park. All the inhabitants of the village were elated when they heard that on the day after the ceremony, the Royal couple, who were the guests of Mark Firth at Oakbrook, were to drive through Crookes in open carriages. The villagers hurriedly put out flags and decorations and waited for the Prince and Princess to arrive.

Unfortunately, when the carriages passed through, the Princess was not amongst the party. This caused great disappointment until a philosophical old lady was heard to remark 'Well, never mind, I know 'ow it is. There was a party at Oakbrook, yer know, last night, and I've no doubt the Princess is stoppin' behind to help Mrs Firth wi' the washin' up!'

In 1887 a Bronze Age cinerary urn, containing human bones, a small cup and a damaged bronze knife, was found in the ground near old Tinker Lane. This lane leads from the top of Crookes towards Rivelin.

Near the place of this find was St Antony's Well, which was believed to have medicinal properties. St Antony is the patron saint of swineherds and, of course, this neighbourhood, with its oak forests, was ideal for the feeding of pigs. The custom was that one pig from each litter was vowed to the saint.

Very little is left today of the old Crookes and many of the roads, including the main street, are now lined with brand new houses and flats.

Walkley

The name of the former village of Walkley comes from the Old English 'Walca's Leah' meaning Walca's forest clearing.

Because the village was built on the side of a steep hill, bleak and open to the continuous winds blowing across the Rivelin valley, the people of Walkley, like those of Crookes, were a hardy and healthy folk.

Near where Heavygate Road now runs, was a fine house called Walkley Hall, probably built by William Rawson about 1600. The Hall was demolished by the Sheffield Corporation in January, 1926, to make way for the present housing estate.

In 1637 the area where Bell Hagg Road now is, was a large open common of about 80 acres. Onto this land the owners of the little farms at Crookes and Walkley turned their cattle in the summer. The name Bell Hagg comes from the Old Norse 'Bale or Belle-Hagi' meaning a fire common.

One of the interesting buildings still standing in Walkley is the old Heavygate Inn. This was built in 1696 and has walls two feet thick. In 1896, to celebrate the 200th anniversary of the opening of the inn, a sheep was roasted in the yard and all who passed that day were given a free sandwich and a drink. It is only to be imagined that more than the usual number of people passed by on that particular day!

John Ruskin, the famous art collector and critic, bought a house overlooking the Rivelin valley, which he converted into a museum to house his fine collection

Tram Terminus, Walkley.

Barber Nook House, Walkley, built in 1728.

of works of art and other objects. The collection was later transferred to Meersbrook Hall, a former home of the noted Shore family. Ruskin House, the building that housed Ruskin's collection at Walkley, still stands, though it was altered considerably when it was converted into a 'Girls' Home'.

In the year 1880 many of the residents of Walkley became worried by a prediction that a volcano would suddenly erupt there on a certain day. Great damage to the area was prophesied! However, much to the disappointment of many of the people, when the time came for the eruption nothing happened and so an alternative entertainment was provided. A man who prided himself on his sense of humour, obtained a wheelbarrow, filled it with tar and set it alight. He then sent the blazing barrow careering down Blake Street, which is a very steep hill. It needs little imagination to think of the commotion this incident caused!

The main road leading into Walkley is Barber Road and this acquired its name from the Barber family who resided at Barber Nook House, a pleasant little cottage built in 1728, and still standing just off the main road behind the Co-operative Store.

Nearby is an area of very fine houses and gardens called Birkendale. This name was derived from the German 'Birkenthal' meaning a valley of birch trees.

Ecclesall

The name Ecclesall probably derives from 'Heeksel-Hallr' meaning the witches' hill, or slope. That this area had association with witches and their like is shown also in the name Dobbin Hill, which comes from the northern word 'Dobby' meaning a goblin. Also, of course, nearby Endcliffe was the elf cliff or bank.

No mention of Ecclesall is made in the Domesday Book, but in the time of King John, about the time when Gerard de Furnival married the great heiress of Hallamshire, Maud de Lovetot, there appears on the scene Ralph de Ecclesall, who had settled in this district. Ralph gave much of his land to the monks of Beauchief and when he died he was buried at the Abbey.

His son was Sir Robert de Ecclesall and he confirmed his father's grants to Beauchief. Sir Robert's son was called Ralph after his grandfather and he was also a knight of the realm. It was he who gave to Beauchief Abbey his mill on the Sheaf, from which comes the district known as the Mill Houses.

Ecclesall had a very ancient chapel built in 1046. It was a small, low building, consisting of two parts, a nave and a chancel. There was a small shed at the west end that contained a bell.

The monks of Beauchief took service in the chapel, to which there was a pleasant walk over the fields. The services were discontinued on the Dissolution of the Monasteries and no further service was held there until 1622. At that time the chapel was restored by the walls being rebuilt, a floor was laid in the chancel and pews set

Ecclesall Church, 1839.

Hunter's Bar, Ecclesall Road, 1880.

up. A pulpit, communion table and new glazed window were also installed. A small wooden steeple was erected on the chapel roof.

This chapel was the only place of worship for the people of Ecclesall until 1788. In that year a new church was built, near the old building, on a spot called CARTER-KNOLL (Carterknowle). The old chapel was then demolished. There has never been a village of Ecclesall, it has always been a scattered district. Even as late as 1723 there were only one and a half persons to the acre!

In 1796 Ecclesall contained 1,071 houses and in 1811 the population was only 6,569 people. Most of the inhabitants were engaged in agriculture, though some worked for the manufacturers of Sheffield. A number of people were employed at Wilson's Snuff Mill, which still exists just off Ecclesall Road.

Around this time the poor people of this district received £7.14.0 (£7.70) annually, the money being subscribed by several benefactors. There were also bequests for the education of poor children.

Most of the south-west corner of the area, was and still is, occupied by Ecclesall Woods, formerly the property of the Earl Fitzwilliam, who was also Lord of the Manor.

In these extensive woods, at the Beauchief side, just off Whirlowdale Road, is a gravestone in memory of a charcoal burner who died in his cabin when it caught fire one night. The charcoal burners or 'wood colliers' as they were known, came mostly from the east end of Sheffield. They would make and light their 'stacks' on a Sunday, so that they could have the charcoal to sell to the steel works the following Friday or Saturday, and so get paid.

The inscription on the gravestone reads:

In Memory
of George Yardley
wood collier, he was burnt
to death in his cabbin on this place
Octr 11th, 1786.
William Brooke, salesman;
David Glossop, gamekeeper;
Thomas Smith, beesome maker;
Sampson Brookshaw, innkeeper.

The last four names of the inscription were friends of the charcoal burner and it was they who erected the gravestone. The first is probably that of the woodman who sold the wood for charcoal burning to those who wanted it; the gamekeeper must have regularly come across Yardley when on his work in the woods; the beesome maker would probably have carried on his craft close by; and the innkeeper was landlord of the Rising Sun, a nearby public house with a very ancient history.

To the north west of Ecclesall lies Whiteley Woods, a name that is derived from 'Hwit-Leah-Wudu' meaning a bright, fair clearing.

Here was situated Whiteley Wood Hall, originally the home of the Ashton family. From them it passed to the Pegges of Beauchief, who sold it to Thomas Boulsover, the inventor of Sheffield Plate. After Boulsover died, the house became the property of William Hutton then, by marriage, it passed to the Silcock family. It is interesting to note that it was a member of this family, Phoebe Silcock, who subscribed the money to build the beautiful Christ Church at Fulwood.

The name of FULWOOD comes from the, Anglo-Saxon 'Ful-Wudu' meaning a wet, marshy woodland. This was, in ancient times, a vast pasturage forest, abounding with trees of fine growth. Here Thomas, Lord Furnival, granted to the Canons of Beauchief Abbey 'common of pasture in his free chaces of Folewode and Ryvelingdene everywhere, sufficient for all their cattle, except goats'.

The old Lords of Sheffield, however, also reserved part of this domain for the pleasures of the chase and it was probably here and in Rivelin, that Robin Hood (or Locksley) made some of his first attempts at 'chasing the fallow deer'. This area lies not very far from Loxley, the legendary home and birthplace of the famous outlaw. This is borne out by the historian Dodsworth, who in 1620 wrote:

> *Robin Locksley, born in Bradfield parish in Hallamshire, wounded his stepfather to death at plough, fled into the woods, and was relieved by his mother till he was discovered. Then he came to Clifton upon Calder, and became acquainted with Little John, that kept the kine* [cow]. *Which said John is buried at Hathershead in Derbyshire, where he hath a fair tombstone with an inscription. Little John was Earl Huntley's son. Afterwards he joined with Much the Millar's son...*

To protect the deer in Fulwood and Rivelin, keepers were appointed by the lords of the manor. The head keeper was known as 'Master of the Game' and each man received the princely salary of £2 per year. However, after the time of Charles I, there was so little game left in the area that the posts of keeper were discontinued.

In 1666, which was a period when people were very alarmed at the spread of the plague, Fulwood Spa was a popular resort. This was a spring of mineral water which, in time, was covered by Thomas Heaton with a building, thus converting it into a spa. Many Sheffield people then visited Fulwood to 'take the waters'.

The spa was situated near the ancient Fulwood Chapel, built in 1729. In front of the chapel, in the small garden, can be seen the stocks which formerly stood on the village green.

There are many old buildings in the Fulwood area, the most noticeable being Fulwood Hall, a building mentioned in deeds of the time of Henry VII.

Today most of Fulwood is a district of fine, large houses, built mostly during the Victorian period, by the rich industrialists of Sheffield. It is a beautiful area and this is reflected in some of the street names, such as 'Hangingwater', meaning a deep, slow-moving stream.

Fulwood Hall, built 1620.

Fulwood Church, 1988.

Fulwood Stocks.

Endcliffe Hall, 1986.

One of the ancient esquire seats in the manor of Ecclesall was BANNER CROSS, a name that comes from the old French 'Baneur', meaning a standard bearer. At the time of Elizabeth I this was called the Banner Field and here was situated the home of the Bright family.

When the Brights became extinct in 1748, the grand-daughter and heiress, Mary Dalton, conveyed the estate to her husband, Lord John Murray of the house of Athol. During his occupation Lord John made many improvements to the hall. However, when it came into the hands of General Murray, he practically demolished the building and, with the assistance of Sir Jeffry Wyatville,[9] he erected the present Banner Cross Hall.

The Scottish names of many of the streets of this area reflect the influence of the Murray family, who came from Tullibardine Castle.

Sir John Murray brought with him to Banner Cross many servants and amongst them was a man called Wragg and his wife. These people were housed in the old Dove Cottages, now demolished, which stood on the site of the present Louth Road. Mr and Mrs Wragg had a daughter, called Molly, who went into service and eventually came to settle down as a midwife and nurse in a little cottage at the top end of Brincliffe Edge. Molly was looked upon as a curer of all ills, so, when anyone was sick, the cry was always 'Fetch Molly Wragg!' Because of this Brincliffe Edge Road was locally known to all as 'Molly Wragg Lane'.

To the north of Ecclesall lies ENDCLIFFE, which was originally called 'Elcliffe', meaning Elf Cliff or Bank. The name is at least as old as 1333 when it was mentioned in a grant to a certain John de Elcliffe.

Dore

The name of Dore is derived from the Anglo Saxon 'Dor' meaning a door, pass or entrance into the kingdom of Mercia.

It is a very ancient village, for here in the year 829, Ecgbert King of Mercia held a meeting with Eanred, King of Northumbria. The result of this was that Ecgbert was declared King of all the English and the Kingdom of England emerged.

The Anglo-Saxon Chronicle from which so much early history is obtained, relates the incident as follows:

> *And Ecgbert led an army to Dore against the Northumbrians and they offered him obedience and concord, and thereupon they separated.*

Ecgbert then became 'Our Lord of the whole English speaking race from the Channel to the Firth of Forth'.

In 1968, 1,139 years after this historic event, a commemorative plaque attached to a large stone, was erected on Dore village green.

King Ecgbert's Stone on the Village Green, Dore.

The Limb Mill at Dore, 1873.

Croft House Farm, Dore.

Cottages at Dore.

Hare and Hounds Public House, Dore.

Totley Old School, built in 1877.

In ancient times the only road from Abbeydale to the village was an old pack-horse lane which skirted Ashfurlong and came out at the top of the hill into what is now the main road. Even at the time of the Commons Enclosure, which took place in Dore from 1809 to 1822, there was only one road from Whirlow Bridge to Totley. This was the only cart road from Sheffield into Dore.

Though mostly agricultural land, the village was also well known for supplying coal to the lead smelters who brought their lead from all parts of Derbyshire to the water-powered smelting cupolas. There were many water-wheels in the area, a number of which powered corn mills in Ryecroft Glen, Barber Field and Old Hay.

The people of Dore were employed in various trades, including button makers, saw and anvil makers, file cutters, boot and shoe makers and of course, agriculture. The Parish Church for this district was at Dronfield, but a small Chapel of Ease was erected at Dore, probably around 1530.

There is an amusing story relating to a man called Frank Parker who was curate of the village for some years previous to 1836. Mr Parker lived in Sheffield town and only came over to Dore on Sundays to take the service. On his visits he was often accompanied by a friend called Jeeves and after the service they would dine at the Hare and Hounds. It is said that if the sermon happened to drag on too long, Mr Jeeves would go to the pulpit steps, tug at Mr Parker's gown, and in a very loud whisper would say 'Frank, Frank, t' goose'll be ready—cut it short, man!' The old Chapel of Ease was demolished in 1828 when the present church was built.

Another interesting character of Dore was Richard Furness, who was not only schoolmaster, but also overseer, architect, scribe, lawyer, doctor, singer, poet and surveyor. A poem describing his various talents went as follows:

I, Richard Furness, Schoolmaster, of Dore,
Keep parish books and pay the poor;
Draw plans for buildings, and indite
Letters for those who cannot write;
Make wills and recommend a proctor,
Cure wounds, let blood with any doctor;
Draw teeth, sing psalms, the hautboy play
At chapel on each holy day;
Paint sign boards, cart names at command,
Survey and plot estates of land;
Collect at Easter, one in ten,
And on the Sunday say—Amen!

In the 19th century Dore was still a small, straggling village with about 500 inhabitants. One of its fine old buildings was Dore Hall, which was owned by Ralph Barker in the 14th century. The hall is described as a fine mansion, with beautiful oak panelling and decorated plaster ceilings. Unfortunately, the hall was demolished in 1840.

Beauchief Abbey, built in 1183.

Beauchief Hall, built in 1671.

Old Cottages at Beauchief.

Remains of Mill Houses.

Today much of the old village has been destroyed, and modern houses, shops and schools spread out across the once open fields.

To the south of Dore is the former hamlet of TOTLEY. It was called in the Domesday Book 'Totingelei', a name meaning a spy or watching place. 'Toting hills' are often met with in early literature, in all cases they were places of defence. Totley being situated on the summit of a steep hill would be an ideal place from which to spy out the land and watch for enemy movements.

Beauchief

Beauchief was the name given by the Norman monks to the area in which they built their Abbey. It means 'beautiful headland' and refers to the delightful surrounding countryside.

The Abbey was founded by Robert Fitz Ranulf, probably in about 1183. It was dedicated to Archbishop Beckett and the Virgin Mary, and was given to the White Canons, some of whom came from Welbeck to settle at Beauchief.

The Abbey continued to function until the Dissolution, in 1537, when it was surrendered to King Henry VIII. Many of the stones from the Abbey were used to build the beautiful Beauchief Hall, situated a short distance away.

At Beauchief can also be seen a reconstructed 18th-century industrial hamlet, the Abbeydale Works. At this museum of one of Sheffield's oldest industries, it is possible to trace the manufacture of steel edge tools from the raw materials to the finished product. Both the forging and grinding machinery were worked by water-wheels and these have been carefully reconstructed to illustrate the working practices of those early days.

Millhouses

As mentioned previously, this name comes from the Corn Mill on the River Sheaf which was given by Ralph de Ecclesall to the monks of Beauchief. It was then known as the Miln Houses or Mill Houses.

In the 12th and 13th centuries the mighty forests of Barnsdale covered most of the land around this area, and here lurked many bands of outlaws to hunt the King's deer. The River Sheaf had many fine trout and these must often have furnished a good meal at the Abbey on Fridays.

In the middle 1800s there were only 23 houses and a few dilapidated file cutters' shops here. There were also, at this time, seven small coal pits within a mile radius, in which implements used by the monks of Beauchief were found.

Apart from the old mill, the Robin Hood Inn and the cottages, the only other building was the Waggon and Horses, a very ancient inn which was probably a farmstead in its earlier days.

Wagon and Horses Public House, Millhouses.

Broadfield Toll Bar, Abbeydale Road, 1830.

Machon Bank, Nether Edge, 1873.

Old London Road, Highfield.

Abbeydale

Abbeydale derives its name from the 'dale of the Abbey' or Abbey-Dale'.

It has never been a village, but simply a valley near the River Sheaf, and was, up to the middle 19th century, completely rural. From the Royal Hotel at the end of Highfield there were practically no houses on Abbeydale Road, with the exception of Broadfield Toll Bar, until Millhouses.

A pleasant mansion later situated in the dale was Abbeydale House. It was built by Joseph Rodgers, founder of the great cutlery firm of that name. This splendid mansion was completely ruined by the erection of a brick-built laundry that occupies the whole of the front grounds and is attached to the front of the house. The house is at present empty and in a very dilapidated state. Adjoining this house and estate was the Broadfield Park Estate, once owned by the Shore family and later by the Shirecliffes.

Of this latter family it was said that there was 'no holding one of the daughters'. We are not told of her misdeeds, but when she died her father was determined that she should now 'be held' if weight of stone could accomplish it. He had her buried at Heeley Church and a large team of horses had a heavy task to drag the weighty tombstone to the churchyard to 'pin down' this lively lady!

Broadfield Toll Bar was so called because it was situated at the top end of the Broad Field, the only reminder of this field now being the road of the same name. The Bar was erected in 1812, when the Abbeydale Road was constructed. A pleasant country path led from the toll bar to Little London Lane at Heeley. It was bordered by a row of fine trees and overlooked the beautiful Primrose Meadows. When this land was developed for housing, many people complained about the destruction of the trees, but, just as today, it was to no avail.

Remains of the ancient country footpaths still exist. One runs from Abbeydale Road to Chesterfield Road and the other from Broadfield Road to Little London Road.

Between Abbeydale and Ecclesall lies NETHER EDGE, a once rural area that was developed by George Wostenholm, the cutlery manufacturer. Wostenholm commenced buying land in this district in 1836, eventually owning most of the land from Brincliffe Edge down to London Road. Upon this land, Wostenholm and Thomas Steade built the fine Nether Edge Estate, comprising mostly detached villas in large gardens. Basing the estate on the American town of Boston, Massachusetts, trees were planted at the sides of all the roads, thus leaving a fine heritage for the occupants of the area today.

Adjoining Nether Edge was the mediaeval hamlet of CHERRYTREE, up to comparatively recently a beautiful oasis of little cottages on what is called Cherrytree Road. Unfortunately many of the cottages have now been destroyed.

Heeley Tilt Mill Dam, 1791.

White Lion Inn, Heeley, 1825.

Heeley

Heeley derives its name from 'Heah Leah', meaning a high, woodland clearing. It is first mentioned in a charter of 1343, when it was called 'Heghlegh'. In 1348 it was spelled 'Heghelegh' and in 1451 it is referred to as 'Hamelet-de-Heyle'. However, in 1553, the spelling is as it appears today.

The village of Heeley nestled on the hillside around the church and green. As the village grew it split into Upper, Middle and Nether Heeley, this latter part now being better known as 'Heeley Bottom'. In the 19th century, where the unused Heeley Railway Station now stands, was a large sheet of water and here horse teams bringing their loads to town would stop to drink.

Near the bridge over the Sheaf, first erected in 1567, stood the Heeley Tilt and from there a thickly wooded bank extended to the bridge at Myrtle Road. In this wood, at the beginning of the 19th century, a murder was committed, the perpetrator of which was executed at York Castle. All around this area were pasture lands and cornfields which extended across to East Bank and The Farm.[10]

The spot near Heeley Toll Bar, commonly called 'Heeley Gates' was noted for many daring robberies. Records tell us that 'In 1839, about 8 o'clock at night, Robert Turner of Bole Hill, Norton, was stopped by five ruffians, who took his hat, umbrella and 15/- in money'. On another evening, a man called Trickett, a fish dealer, was stopped and robbed by several men of 5/6.

Just off Gleadless Road, behind where the Shakespeare Hotel now stands, was Heeley Hall, an ancient 15th-century building. All traces of this hall have now disappeared.

Many interesting field names existed in this area, including one called 'Two Days Work'. This was mentioned in a document of 1663—obviously this must have been an exceptionally large field.[11]

At the end of Oak Street used to stand a whitewashed farmhouse surrounded by corn fields, though this was demolished many years ago. In a wall that used to surround the now demolished Oak Street Church, was fixed a date stone on which were carved the initials A.I.M. and the date 1717. This stone came from a cottage which was knocked down to make way for the widening of Gleadless Road. The old stone, along with the wall, was destroyed by the bulldozers which completely flattened this part of Heeley during 1970.

Heeley Church was opened in 1848, and there was a school erected in 1833, endowed with lands amounting to about £20 a year.

In the churchyard is a granite memorial to J. Shortridge of Chipping House.[12] It was he who built the railway from Sheffield to Manchester and who was responsible for the Wicker Arches.

There were many wells and springs at Heeley and these are remembered in the names, Well Road, Well Head Road and Springwood Road. At the bottom of

Old Red Lion Inn, Heeley, 1876.

The Gleadless Valley Estate.

Bishops House, Meersbrook Park.

Meersbrook House, 1894.

Well Road there existed a 'Catch Bar' this was erected to prevent travellers evading the Heeley Toll Bar.

The beginning of the changes that led to the Heeley of the present day, began with the draining of the Little London Dam to make way for the Midland Railway. Then the Hardy Patent Pick Company and Sir Charles Skelton's shovel works opened up new fields of industry, bringing with them an influx of workers. These workers required to live close at hand and so houses were built all around the works. Street after street gradually thrust over the hillside and, to meet the requirements of the new population, enterprising shopkeepers opened up businesses all along the main road.

To the south east of Heeley was the straggling village of GLEADLESS, a name which comes from the Old English 'Glida Leah', meaning a kite clearing in a wood. All the farms and most of the cottages of Gleadless have now disappeared, modern houses and shops taking their place.

The Gleadless Valley, formerly a beautiful stretch of open countryside and woodland extending from Heeley to Norton, now houses what was in the 1970s 'the show estate' of Sheffield. Unusually good planning of the streets and houses on the contours of the valley has preserved a number of open spaces and trees which would otherwise have been destroyed.

To the north east of Gleadless lies HOLLINSEND, formerly a straggling hamlet of small cottages and farms. Here there existed two of the oldest cottages in the Sheffield area. Built in the 15th century, these picturesque homes were, some years ago, stated to be 'unfit for human habitation' and were demolished. Referring to the buildings being unfit for human habitation, it should be noted that one of the cottages was occupied by the Crouch family for many generations and all the members of that family died at a ripe old age. The last tenant was Mr Joe Crouch who died in 1962 at the age of 82!

To the east of Hollinsend is situated HACKENTHORPE, the name meaning 'Hachen's outlying farmstead'. In 1860 this was a village of sickle manufacturers, 30,000 dozen being made each year. One of the largest employers of labour in this area was Thomas Staniforth of Darnall. Nearby is BIRLEY SPA, named after a spring of mineral water that was found very beneficial to health. Earl Manvers, the owner of the district, empowered a committee of four gentlemen to erect a large establishment of seven baths, for the use of the public, in 1843. As it was pointed out at the time, the Spa was 'situated in a sylvan and rural glen, entirely surrounded by romantic hills, tastefully laid out and planted'. Now, of course, Birley Spa is surrounded by a large, modern housing estate.

To the south of Heeley is MEERSBROOK, a name derived from the stream called the Meers Brook that runs down from Norton Lees until it meets the River Sheaf at Saxon Bridge, Heeley. The Meers Brook means a 'boundary brook' and it and the Sheaf formed part of a frontier line between the ancient kingdoms of Northumbria

The Dale Farm, Woodseats.

Path to Barber's Fields, Dale Farm, Woodseats.

and Mercia. Up to comparatively modern times this brook was also the boundary between Yorkshire and Derbyshire.

At the top of Meersbrook Park, at NORTON LEES, is one of Sheffield's oldest houses, the Bishop's House. Built probably in the 16th century, it acquired its name from the two bishops of the Blythe family, John and Geoffrey.

Up to the middle of the nineteenth century the road from Meersbrook to Woodseats was completely rural and very sparsely populated. On each side of the road was Smithy Wood, which extended from the River Sheaf to the top of Scarsdale Road, formerly called Green Lane.

Woodseats

The inhabitants of Woodseats or Norton Woodseats, from the Old English 'Wodesettes' or 'Wodesete', meaning a fold in wood, were in ancient times mostly occupied in assisting the monks of Beauchief Abbey with their agriculture.

Most of old Woodseats was clustered around a farmstead near a little narrow lane called The Dale. All the old cottages and the farm have now been demolished.

Other cottages existed along what is now Chesterfield Road and near the Cold Brook, opposite Cobnar Road. Here also, was a farm belonging to a man called Jonathon Booth, and it is recorded that John Wesley stopped and preached a sermon here, as he passed through Woodseats in the year 1753. At the top of Cobnar Road is Bole Hill, an ancient way still unfit for motor traffic.[13]

The little school that still stands at the bottom of Cobnar Road was erected by Charles Cammell in 1861. Charles Cammell lived at Norton Hall and the estate and grounds of this fine house are now known as Graves Park. This beautiful park extends from Norton to Woodseats and covers an area of two hundred and six acres. The park acquired its name from Alderman J.G. Graves, who presented the estate to the City in 1925.

The original Big Tree Inn, so called from the tree growing in the forecourt, was a stop for the horse-drawn coaches on their three-day journey to London. The present inn is the second one on this site, the tree is the third, the first was split down the centre by an elephant.

Norton

The name of Norton is derived from 'Nord-Tun', meaning the north farmstead.

It was first mentioned in the will of Wulfric Spott, who appears to have been an officer attached to the court of King Ethelred in 1002.

The Manor of Norton at the time of Edward the Confessor, belonged to Godeva and Nada. Afterwards it passed through the families of de Busli, Fitz Ranulph, Chaworth, Ormond, Dynham, Babington and others, until it came into the hands of the Offleys, from whom it passed to Samuel Shore, of Norton Hall.

Woodseats Cinema, built in 1911.

Old Cottages, Cartmell Road, Woodseats.

St James Church, Norton, 1992.

The Oakes, Oakes Park, Norton, built in 1672.

Norton Grange, built in 1744. Now 'Chantreyland Nursery School'.

The old Norton village was a picturesque place, described in one record as follows:

> *Norton is interesting and pleasant, the cottages are generally plain, but being embosomed in gardens, festooned with roses, or overhung with trees, present an unusual air of comfort and repose.*

The lovely church of St James, dating from Saxon times, was bestowed upon Beauchief Abbey by Robert Fitz Ranulph, Lord of Norton, between 1172 and 1176.

An elegant feature of this church is the Blythe chapel, built in 1520, in which is the tomb of the Blythe family. The Blythes lived in the previously mentioned Bishop's House at Norton Lees.

When restorations were made to the church in 1882, a memorial stone dated 1674, which lay under the altar adjoining the east window, was found to tell the unusual story of Barbara Lee. It appears this good lady was buried under or near the fireplace, which was then situated on the site of the altar. The body was buried upright in a perpendicular hole, with the fireplace over the head. It is said that this may have been done for a particular reason, but probably there was no room to lay the coffin in the usual position.

Both in the church and in the churchyard are many monuments to notable Norton families, including the Bullocks, Eyres, Morewoods, Gills, Clarkes, Shores and Bagshawes. The grave of Sir Francis Chantrey can be seen just outside the old church porch.

Many of the gravestones have been lost or broken quite recently in an unnecessary 'tidying up' of the churchyard. One old stone had the following inscription in memory of a blacksmith who lived and worked near the top of Meadowhead:

> *Mark Tyzack, of Four Lane Ends,*
> *Blacksmith, Buried in 1795.*
> *My scythe and hammer lies reclin'd;*
> *My bellows too, have lost their winde;*
> *My iron is spent, my steel is gone;*
> *My scythes are set, my work is done;*
> *My fire extinct, my forge decay'd;*
> *My body in the dust is laid.*

Near the church, on a small piece of grass that is all that is left of the village green, stands an obelisk of Cheesewing granite, a memorial to Sir Francis Chantrey, erected by public subscription in 1854.

In the 17th and 18th centuries, several fine houses were erected in and around the village, most of which still stand today. These include Norton Hall, the Parsonage, Norton Grange and the Oakes.

Norton hall, built 1815.

Chantrey's Cottage where he was born in 1781.

Chantrey's School in School Lane, Norton.

Chantrey's Monument on the Village Green.

Old Norton Post Office, School Lane.

Jordanthorpe Hall Farm, Cinderhill Lane.

The only public house, complete with a large bowling green, was at MAGATHAY (wrongly called MAUGERHAY today) a picturesque hamlet that clustered around the inn. Here was an ancient field with the unusual name of 'Plackling Magatha'. The name came from the Anglo Saxon 'Placke', meaning an open space and the second part is obviously a shortened form of Magathay.

At HEMSWORTH nailmakers lived and worked in their small cottages around an inn—the Nailmaker's Arms. The licence for this public house was granted in 1626. Nearby was a farmstead that later became the Bagshawe Arms and it is interesting to note that, in the 19th century, an outbuilding of this public house was used as the Petty Sessions Court, held every second Wednesday of the month.

Among the many old superstitions adhered to by the farmers of this area was one that required a pig's hock being hung up in the farmhouse. This hock had to be whitewashed every time the house was whitewashed and this was believed to protect the cattle from disease!

To the south of Norton Church was the small hamlet of JORDANTHORPE, a name of Danish origin meaning Jourdain's outlying farmstead. Here, Sir Francis Chantrey, one of England's most famous sculptors, was born in 1781.

Of the old buildings, only Jordanthorpe Hall, Chantrey's Cottage and Jordanthorpe Hall Farm remain.

Cinderhill Lane, on the side of which all these buildings stand, was, even in recent times, extremely beautiful. Here it was possible to wander between hedgerows of wild flowers, to see for miles across unspoiled countryside and to have one's ears filled with birdsong. Occasionally, from the nearby woods of Hazlebarrow, could be heard the barking of a dog fox and hares could be observed scampering across the fields.

However, in 1969 the bulldozers arrived, the ancient hedgerows were ripped from the ground and within a few months modern houses were covering the scene. Cinderhill Lane then became just another piece of suburbia. But worse was to come, for a giant, ugly electricity sub-station was built in the fields behind the old farm!

Though Norton managed to keep its rural aspect longer than most of Sheffield's suburbs, the tentacles of development are now gripping it tightly and modernity is quickly taking over. The cottages of Magathay have been reduced to rubble, huge housing estates creep over the grazing lands toward Hazlebarrow and even the beautiful Oakes Park is threatened.

To Norton, then, farewell,
The homes, the church upon the village green,
Old thoughts that circle like the birds of even'
Round the grey tower. Soft, sweet regrets, like sunset
Lighting old windows with gleams day had not,
Ghosts of dead years, whispering old names
Through the grass grown pathways and age-old trees.

NOTES

1. John Harrison in his survey of 1637 writes 'The chiefest ffishinge within the manno is the rivers that passeth through the same wherein are a great store of salmons, trouts, chevens [chub], celes, and other small fish'.

2. On September 29th, 1785, it was resolved at a meeting held in Sheffield, to erect a commodious inn on the site 'where the Castle Barns now stand' at a cost of not less than £4,000, this sum to be raised by a tontine. There were 50 subscribers of £100 each, including the Earl of Surrey, who took five shares. Each subscription nominated a life, during the continuance of which he was to receive an equal share of the rents and profits.

   The Tontine was a great posting or coaching house and there were always twenty horses and five post boys ready when the yard bell rang and the call given 'First pair out!'

   At one time the host had as many as 300 horses standing at different staging posts. However, when the railways arrived the whole posting establishment collapsed and all the horses were sold, no matter what the price.

   In 1890, the Duke of Norfolk purchased the Tontine Inn for £7,720 so that he could demolish it to erect the Norfolk Market Hall on the site. A large store now stands upon the spot where the famous coaching inn was erected at the corner of Haymarket and Dixon Lane.

3. 'Till mor ship lands at t'bottom o' Park Hill' obviously derived from the days of the merchant adventurers, whose common remark was 'Wait until my ship comes in!'

4. In the 18th century hanging was the usual punishment for the crime of stealing. A person could also be hanged for picking pockets if more than one shilling (5p) was taken! It was also a hanging matter for stealing goods worth more than five shillings from a shop. In Sheffield it was a common occurrence, as a minor punishment, to be put in a cart and whipped on the bare shoulders as the cart proceeded from the Church Gates down to Lady's Bridge.

5. This large park covered about 2,500 acres and reached from the River Sheaf (near what is now the Sheffield Railway Station) to Gleadless Town End. It was full of magnificent oak trees, mostly cut down in the 17th and 18th centuries. The Manor Lodge was built in the midst of this park by George, 4th Earl of Shrewsbury, early in the reign of Henry VIII. There was just one private road through the park, with gates at each entrance.

6. Bat, stick and trip refers to the ancient game of 'Peggy' which was rather similar to Knur and Spell. This game was common some sixty years ago and the author remembers playing

Peggy for many hours when a boy. The 'bat' consisted of a thick stick of wood, the 'stick' was a small piece of wood laid on the ground and the 'trip' was a further short piece sharpened at both ends. The trip was laid partly across the stick, the end of the trip was then sharply hit with the bat, causing it to spring about three feet into the air. This had then to be hit again as hard as possible. The distance between the batter and where the trip fell had then to be paced out, and naturally, the winner was the person who had hit the trip the longest distance.

Obviously the Methodist minister was pointing out to young Mather that he who played games on a Sunday was 'on the wrong road', 'The road to Loxley Edge' refers to what happened to the murderer, Frank Fern, who was gibbeted on this bleak common.

7. The ancient family, of good yeoman stock, is directly connected with the author's family. This happened when William Vickers married Elizabeth Twybell of Southey, in the middle of the 18th century. The author is a direct descendant of William and Elizabeth. From William Vickers' brother John, came Edward Vickers, who became the head of the famous Don Steel Works—Vickers & Company.

8. The sticking of pins or bodkins into the mantelpiece by guests, seems to have been a common practice in those days. The reason for this ancient custom is, however, lost in antiquity.

9. This famous architect was born plain Jeffry Wyatt, on August 3rd, 1766, at Burton on Trent. He eventually became the designer of over 100 buildings, among which are the north wing of Chatsworth House, and the entrance and various additions to Longleat. However, he is best known for his work on Windsor Castle, started in 1824. For this, King George IV bestowed on him a knighthood, he was allowed to alter his name to Wyatville and he was given a residence in the Winchester Tower. Sir Jeffry died on February 10th, 1840, in London. A portrait of him, painted by Sir Francis Chantrey, is in the National Portrait Gallery.

10. This was a mansion that was formerly the Sheffield home of the Duke of Norfolk and his agent. It was rebuilt in 1824, the dining room having a ceiling copied from the one in the 'Mary, Queen of Scots Room' at the Manor Lodge. The very fine grounds were spoilt when the Midland Railway was constructed. The mansion has now been demolished, it stood where McDonald's is today at the corner of Farm Road and Granville Road.

11. Fairbanks recorded many of the ancient field names in the Sheffield area, including the following. At Tinsley: Swan Nest, Cinquefoil Close, Arcos, Freezeland Close, Plonk Holme and Temple Bank. At Darnall: Bessy Meadow, Fiddle Case, Great Tongue, In the Hades and Pogonore Land. In Attercliffe: Castle Meadow, Goodman Storth, Herring Field, Long Hades, Mountney Field, Mag Field, Partridge. Flatt, Slattering Rig, Stacye Field and Lamb Pool (Jansen Street, off Attercliffe Common, was originally called Lamb Pool Lane). At Dore: Crude Sick, America, Floated Field, Savage Acres, Saint Igna, Wag Wood, Tippy Lands and Maiden's Hillock.

12. This was a mansion that stood on the site of the present Chippinghouse Road at Abbeydale. Steade Road, Brookfield Road and St Ronan's Road were laid out on the grounds of Chipping House.

13. Bole Hills were places where iron was smelted in open wood furnaces, they were always situated at the top of a hill to ensure a good draught. There are Bole Hills at Crookes and other places around the city.

The Head Post Office, 1996.

PART 3

A PHOTOGRAPHIC VIEW OF SHEFFIELD IN THE 1990s

The Town Hall from the Peace Gardens, 1996.

Town Hall Square with Goodwin Fountain, 1996.

High Street, 1996.

Barkers Pool with War Memorial, 1996.

The City Hall, 1996.

Fargate, 1996.

View across Castle Square, 1996.

Graves Art Gallery and Library, 1996.

Hallam University, 1999.

The National Centre for Popular Music, Paternoster Row, 1999.

Fountain in the New Peace Gardens, 1999.

PART 4

STORIES, LEGENDS AND ANECDOTES OF OLD SHEFFIELD

Listen and I'll tell you stories
Of ancient Sheffield and its glories,
Of characters that are long dead,
Of ghosts and gibbets and a silver bed!

The Life and Times of Joseph Mather

Joseph Mather was born in 1737, in 'Cack Alley' a gennel which led from Lambert Street to Westbar Green. As a youth he was apprenticed to the file trade in the small works of Nicholas Jackson of Shemeld Croft.

Joseph was only small in stature but rather wide, and for most of his younger days he belonged to the Methodists. From them he acquired a good knowledge of the Bible, from which he frequently quoted.

To earn a few extra coppers, Mather, throughout his life, composed ballads which he sold in the streets and at public houses. Usually when selling his songs, he would ride seated the wrong way round on a grinder's donkey, or sometimes, on the back of a young bull. Should it start to rain he would steer the animal into the nearest alehouse.

Though Mather's moral character was reasonably good, he was easily led astray and quite often he would finish up in the old gaol in Pudding Lane (now King Street). This was a debtor's gaol, of only two cells—one for each sex. Sheffield folk could be sent there for owing as little as sixpence!

The last years of Mather's life were spent in sickness and poverty at his house, now in Pond Hill, and when he died in 1804, at the age of 67, he was buried in St Paul's churchyard. It was fitting that the funeral service should be performed by the Reverend Alexander Mackenzie, for during his life Mather had many times satirised the parson under the title of 'Old Crow'.

The ballads written by Mather symbolised the terrible conditions under which most Sheffield people lived, as the following extract clearly illustrates:

Poverty, that vile tormentor,
Keeps me in strong bonds confined;
Fortune quits me at a venture
Since I've got a generous mind,
Rags disguise me, friends despise me,
Bums and lawyers catechise me,
All against me seem combined.

Chorus

Wearied bones, despised and daunted,
Hungry guts and empty purse,
Hung with rags, by bailiffs haunted,
Prove the times grow worse and worse.

Some of Mather's songs were extremely coarse, especially when they were about some magistrate, clergyman or employer who was disliked by the poorer Sheffield folk. For example, when Mr Watkinson, who was Master Cutler in 1787, demanded the supply of thirteen knives to the dozen, the trade found vent for their indignation through a ballad by Mather, which had the following verse:

Then may the odd knife his great carcase dissect,
Lay open his vitals for men to inspect,
A heart full of black as the infernal gulf,
In that greedy, bloodsucking, bonescraping wolf!

An example of the conditions existing in Sheffield town during Mather's lifetime are expressed in the following poem:

Where slowly down the vale a river runs,
Of dark complexion like its crooked sons;
In a fair country, stands a filthy town,
By bugs and butchers held in high renown;
Sheffield the Black—in ugliness supreme;
Yet ugly Sheffield is my dirty theme.

The poet then goes on to mention the unlovely buildings and the volume of smoke which rises from the town, until the sun 'hangs like a copper shield'. Then when it rains, the writer tells us:

Ah, luckless he, who in unhappy hour
Is doomed to walk our streets beneath the shower,
No friendly spout from the projecting eaves,
The copious tribute of the clouds receives,
But headlong from the roof, in sooty showers,
Prone on the hapless passenger it pours.
While on our moonless evenings, dark and damp,
Imprudent thrift denies the public lamp
And many a dunghill graces many a street.

The poet then refers to the streets of Sheffield after very heavy rain and continues:

Whole streams of rubbish and whole seas of mud;
With turnip tops, potato peelings join,
And to their cast garments, peas and beans combine,
Providing pigs and ducks with goodly cheer;
To pigs and ducks our streets are ever dear,
May no audacious scavenger presume to wield the rake, the shovel or the broom!

Customs and Conditions in Old Sheffield Town

An old custom of Sheffield, long since passed into obscurity, was the way of showing respect for the dead by the sending of 'Berring' or burying cakes to the relatives of the deceased. The Berring Cakes were wrapped in white writing paper and sealed with black sealing wax. The larger the size of the cake the greater the respect shown—or so it was assumed.

Joseph Mather wrote a song called *Round Legs* and part of one verse was:

Round Legs to Wadsley went,
With berring cakes he was sent...

Round Legs was the nickname of the man who worked as carrier for a baker's shop.

Legislation against the workers during the 18th century was extremely severe. If a workman refused to work the hours offered, at the rate offered, he was fined £10 and, if he couldn't pay which was usually the case, he got twenty days imprisonment on bread and water. For a second offence the fine was doubled and if he could not pay this he was fastened in the pillory. For a third offence the fine was £46 and in default he was put in the pillory and had one of his ears cut off!

One can appreciate why when, in 1727, advertisements appeared offering great advantages to filesmiths if they would settle in France, the workmen of Sheffield began to dispose of their effects and pack up their tools for the journey. This so worried Judge Jessop of Broom Hall that he petitioned the King, asking him to prevent the departure of the workmen. The King granted the petition.

However, in 1732 a Filesmiths' Benefit Society was established and this was quickly followed by the Cutlers' Carpenters', Grinders', Masons', Braziers' and other societies. These were the forerunners of the trade unions.

The Wesleyan Methodists met with much opposition when they founded their first chapels in Sheffield. In 1743 the little chapel they had built in Pinstone Lane was completely demolished by rioters.

Through the whole of the winter of 1766, Mulberry Street Chapel was repeatedly attacked by ruffians and foul names were hurled at the people entering the building. Women in particular bore the brunt of these attacks and their cloaks and gowns were often slashed with knives.

A favourite trick of the ruffians would be to enter the chapel with a cat or fowl tucked underneath their coats. These would then make loud noises during the service, annoying the preacher and congregation alike.

At one time the objectors to the Methodists climbed up the outside of the chapel to the skylight, which was situated just over the pulpit. There they made such a nuisance of themselves by mimicking the preacher that shutters had to be fixed over the window. After this the rioters threw stones at the locked doors and battered on them with wooden clubs.

The greatest evil in those times was drunkenness and this was not confined just to the poorer classes. Outside many of the public houses were signs reading 'Get drunk for a penny, dead drunk for tuppence and have clean straw for nothing'.

The hours of work for most people were extremely long. In 1759 tailors would work from six o'clock in the morning to eight o'clock in the evening for the princely wage of three shillings (15 pence).

Most of the cutlers' premises were very small, with a shop at the front and a forge in the yard behind. The shop usually entered by a low doorway and down a stone step. Written orders for the chapman, who came round and distributed his favours according to the samples shown, were stuck in the leaden casement of the windows and thereafter formed a subject of comment for the people passing by. The workmen were frequently bandy legged this was said to be due to the cramped position in which they worked.

Street conditions were very bad at this time, most of the narrow lanes and alleys being dirty and badly lit. As one poet wrote:

> *When dingy oil lamps shone at neet,*
> *Like glow worms in a wood;*
> *When we could scarcely pick betweet*
> *The causeway from the mud.*

By the mid nineteenth century conditions for the working people of Sheffield had slightly improved. However, most folk were still poor and there were many beggars, who, more often than not, were women with children.

Very few people bought a newspaper, but would rely for their knowledge of what was going on in the world on the placards placed on the streets by the newspaper publishers.

When children were lost, the mother would chalk on the pavement, 'Lost a little boy of two years. Return to Mrs so and so' or words to that effect.

Poultry was kept in the cellars of many of the houses, the fowls being allowed to roam the streets during the daytime, to scratch for food amongst the rubbish thrown all around.

In the little house-shop windows many delicacies were for sale, including bundles of ha'penny treacle sticks wrapped in brightly coloured paper. Home made butterscotch and forthcakes (treacle parkin) were also on sale. To delight young children there were sheep, cows and dogs made of pastry, with currants for eyes and lemon peel for mouths. It was a common sight to see boys and girls chewing liquorice root or eating the locust bean.

Entertainment in Old Sheffield

The entertainment of Sheffield folk in olden times was often of a violent and brutal nature. Cock fighting was commonplace up to 1830, when the last (official) cock fight took place on the Manor. The same year also saw the last badger baiting in the Hyde Park area. Bull baiting was also a favourite pastime, a bull being firmly chained to a stake fixed in the ground, whilst savage dogs were allowed to attack it. Bull baiting took place in the Haymarket, which was originally called 'Bullstake'. On the Moor rat worrying was a common practice, the contest being to see how many rats could be worried by terriers in a given time.

The well-to-do indulged in fox hunting and there is an amusing story of a hunt that took place in 1804.

It appears that, after a long chase, the huntsmen and hounds of Sir William Chambers Bagshawe, of the Oakes in Norton, had followed the fox into the village of Attercliffe. The fox took refuge in a public house, but the hounds failed to find it and after a time the huntsmen called the dogs off. The following morning it was found that the fox had taken refuge in a large sett pot in the kitchen and as soon as the public house door was opened the fox shot out and was away!

Feasts, or fairs, were the highlight of the year for the working class people and in the *Shevvild Chap's Song Book* one of these is aptly described in verse:

A few months since on frolic bent,
On a journey to Little Sheffield[1] *Feast I went,*
And being as all of your know quite green,
I was mortally pleased with the sights I'd seen:
There was Betty and Jenny and Factory Nan,
And twenty more girls and they each had a man,
And Sally and Sukey, and Bandy-leg'd Jack,
And the chap that sold pies with his can on his back,
There were donkeys and dog-carts, and lots of fine folks,
With their jaws all a cracking their nuts and their jokes,
As hungry as hunters from biggest to least,
All right for a blow out at Little Sheffield Feast.

Football in those days was not quite the same as today. For instance, in 1854 a match took place at Bents Green between Norton and Sheffield. The colours of the Norton men were red, while the Sheffielders wore green.

Before the match began it was noticed that the Sheffield supporters had turned up in such force that it was advisable for the Norton team to send for reinforcements and this they did. As usual after the match, a general battle commenced and many of the Sheffield men, who in those days wore their hair very long and tied in a 'tail', lost this part of their anatomy.

The result of this match and the ensuing fight caused quite a stir and for some days afterwards no Norton man dared show his face in Sheffield town.

Naturally the public houses were the favourite venue of most of the folk and there were very many of these establishments, both large and small, in the town.

Some of the most well known were also coaching inns, and amongst these were the Angel, the Tontine and the King's Head. Of the four ancient public houses that existed in High Street: The Grey Horse, The White Bear, The Bay Childers and The Blue Bell, only the last named remains today and that in name only.

A public house situated in Waingate was called the Rose and Crown. Built in 1813, it was so renowned for its beer that the following poem was composed in honour of the beverage:

The Rose and Crown
In Sheffield town,
The landlord's name George Hartley,
He brews good ale,
It is not stale,
Where 'tis I'll tell you shortly.
It's in Waingate,
Which is not straight,
And leads into the Wicker,
Call as you pass,
And take a glass,
'Twill make you travel quicker!

In the eighteenth and nineteenth centuries many theatres were opened in Sheffield, though theatrical shows were given before that time in a building situated through the yard of the Angel Inn in Angel Street.

One of the early theatres was the Surrey Music Hall, West Bar, one of the first of its kind in the United Kingdom, certainly the most beautiful, and second only to Covent Garden in London. It had a splendid ballroom surrounded by enormous mirrors and magnificent pictures. Unfortunately, fire broke out on March 25th, 1865, and the whole building was gutted. The ruins of this fine theatre remained until 1880, when they were cleared away to permit the building of the Union Offices.

There was also the Alexandra Theatre, usually called the 'Old Alex' which closed in 1914, and the Alhambra, destroyed by fire in 1882. Others, within recent memory, were the Hippodrome, the Theatre Royal, the Albert Hall, the Empire and the Lyceum. The last named is listed as being of historic and architectural interest and has been restored. In 1838 Johann Strauss, the elder, visited Sheffield, and an advertisement in the *Sheffield Mercury* of October 6th stated:

> *Theatre Royal, Sheffield*
>
> *The celebrated Valze Composer from Vienna, with his unrivalled orchestra composed of 28 artistes, begs respectfully to announce a Grand Evenings Concert to take place on Thursday, October 11th, 1838, on which occasion he will introduce a selection of his compositions as performed by him at the Courts of Austria, Prussia, France, Holland, Belgium and at the Coronation in London.*
>
> *Prices of admission—5/-, 2/6d and 1/6d.*

Whether these were special prices is not stated, but it is interesting to note that the following week admission was 3/-, 2/- and 1/-.

During the summertime a favourite resort, especially of the young ladies was the Botanical Gardens. The Gardens were opened in 1836 and occupied eighteen acres of land between Clarkehouse Road and Ecclesall Road. In the good weather 'promenades' were held, when the ladies, dressed in their finery, promenaded, chatted and flirted—all to the musical accompaniment of a band. It was always said at the time that 'though marriages may be made in heaven, many Sheffield marriages were hatched at the Proms!'

Galas were often held in the Botanical Gardens and all kinds of amusements were staged. On one occasion, Blondin, the world-famous tight-rope walker, performed his daring feats above the tree tops. As the prices of admission to these galas were very low, it was not unusual to have crowds of 20,000–30,000 people listening to the music and enjoying the entertainment.

The Odd Characters of Sheffield

> *Mary Ann of Sheffield is my name,*
> *England is my nation,*
> *Sheffield is my place of birth,*
> *And Sheffield my limitation!*

Sheffield of the 19th and early 20th centuries had many famous and odd characters who were well known to all and sundry, usually by their first names or nickname.

There was, for example 'Upsy Daisy' who used to play a concertina in Norfolk Park. It is said this man got his nickname for the time when he saw a small boy fall down in front of a fast moving horse and trap. Running into the road he pulled the child from under the horse's hooves, dusted the boy down and said simply, 'Upsy daisy!'

A man who sold laces and bits of leather for repairing boots, was called 'Tacking Ends', and a coloured man, well known in the East End, was always known as 'Snowball'.

Doctor Durrant

Doctor Durrant was always driven through the streets of Sheffield by a coachman dressed in fine livery. Every few minutes, as they travelled along, the coachman would blow upon a long horn, with the good doctor bawling out 'Blow, Joe, blow!' intermixed with other expletives I dare not mention.

The doctor was very fond of drink and would patronise most of the public houses which were situated on his rounds. Good naturedly, he would ask his coachman what he would have to drink. The wily coachman, who did not believe in drinking ale if he could have something stronger, would always reply 'Same as you, Mester, same as you!'

The Blind Fiddlers

Many blind fiddlers existed in Sheffield in the 19th century and the 'Q in the Corner', a public house in Paradise Square, was a well known resort for these entertainers.

The landlord of the Q in the Corner, Samuel Goodlad, had a very fine memory for music, and he claimed the right to play the first fiddle on all public occasions. He would boast he had all the new tunes from London and played them before any other person.

On one occasion Samuel performed a new tune for the benefit of his customers but was unaware that some men had carried into the public house, hidden inside a sack, a blind fiddler called Stephen.

While Samuel was being congratulated on his playing, the sack was carried out again. Blind Stephen was released and then re-entered the public house, whereupon his conspirators called to him, asking if he could play the tune that Samuel Goodlad said only he knew! Blind Stephen said 'Of course I can, and better than anyone else in the town!' The aggrieved landlord bet him 'a leg of mutton and trimmings' if he could play the tune. The blind fiddler, having an even keener ear for music than Samuel, played the tune perfectly and won the wager!

When Stephen left the Q in the Corner, it was past midnight. He explained to the landlord's new wife, who didn't know that he was blind, that he was not afraid of seeing a ghost, but as it was a dark night, please could he borrow a lantern

The kind-hearted landlady said it was a favour she couldn't deny, so she told a servant girl to get one for him.

Equipped with his lantern the jovial fiddler set off towards Pinstone Lane, but he hadn't gone very far when someone asked the landlady why she had lent a lantern to a blind man. Thinking she would be a laughing stock if word got around, the landlady sent the servant girl after Blind Stephen to retrieve the lantern.

However, Blind Stephen refused to give it up. The girl argued with him, saying how useless a lantern was to a blind man, but Stephen just laughed and said 'Does't think I borrowed it for me sen? Tell thi mistress that there's so many drunken folk in the streets that if one knocked me down and smashed mi fiddle I'd be ruined. I'm much obliged to her for the lantern and though *I* can't see it, others can!'

Blind John and his Wife

Another story of these fiddlers concerns Blind John and his wife. These two were beggars and could always be seen in the neighbourhood of Saville Street and Attercliffe Road. They would beg for money and occasionally sing a hymn to the scrapings of John's fiddle.

On one occasion they had sung five or six verses of a hymn when John ceased playing and inquired of his wife 'Is anybody about?'

'No, John, nob'dy!' was the reply.

'Come along then' grumbled Blind John. 'We can sing "Come to Jesus" till hell fetches us, but if there's nob'dy about, nob'dy 'll gi' us owt!'

Charlie Milner

Charlie Milner had an ironmonger's shop in Fargate. He was a friendly character but, rather like our present politicians, he could never answer a question with a straight yes or no.

One day some grinders made a wager that a straight yes or no could be got from him. Accordingly two of them went to the ironmonger's shop and enquired 'Mr Milner, does a coach go from here to Baslow every day?'

However, the wager was lost, for Charlie instantly replied with a question 'Does tha want to go to Baslow then?'

The Turkey Rhubarb Sellers

These characters used to stand amidst the tripe vendors in King Street. They would keep up a constant barrage of chatter to the crowd, but their favourite spiel was always the same:

> *Real genuine Turkey rhubarb—mine uncle goes to Turkey vonce every year and comes back twice a year. The real genuine Turkey rhubarb!*

People would stand, listen, gaze and wonder, at the rhubarb sellers, meanwhile consuming penn'orths of tripe.

The Compulsive Gambler

William Lee, who lived in High Street in the 18th century, was a well known gambler and a very regular frequenter of the Bay Childers public house. Naturally

Lee made a point of attending all the local races and one day, on his way to Doncaster, he noticed the coach in front swaying very violently.

This coach was carrying Lee's wife and only son but, his betting instinct being so strong, William shouted to his friend sitting beside him 'Five to four that carriage turns over and our John is killed!'

Sequah

Sequah wasn't a Sheffield man, but he was a favourite character with the townsfolk of the late 19th century.

He would come to Sheffield dressed as a cowboy wearing a large Stetson hat. Usually hiring the Drill Hall, he would drive there in a gilt carriage drawn by cream ponies and escorted by a large band of cowboys.

Sequah would then dress as an Indian chief whilst he extracted teeth, cured rheumatism and attended to many other complaints. The cries of the people having their teeth extracted were drowned by a terrific noise made by the cowboy band!

The real name of this showman dentist was Hannaway Rowe and when he retired he went to live in a small herbalist's shop in Southampton. He died in 1934 having reached the ripe old age of ninety-three.

How Grinder Jim received his Foot-ale

Before the advent of steam, most grinding work was carried on at the water-wheels which abounded on all the rivers of Sheffield. In these workshops, or grinding hulls, it was an ancient custom that whenever a workman joined the wheel, got married or had a child, he had to provide money for ale to celebrate the occasion.

In a grinding hull on the River Sheaf, one of the grinders was a young man called Jack Grindleblade, who was courting the pretty daughter of 'Buffing' Bill. The couple had decided to get married at Whitsuntide and when the big day arrived Jack and Molly were wed at the Parish Church in Sheffield. When they came out as man and wife all Jack's workmates were waiting at the church door and the groom soon found himself uncomfortable with his 'neckhole' stuffed full of rice![2]

From the church the couple walked to the home of Molly's father where a fine spread was waiting. As was usual, most of the men had too much to drink, including the bridegroom, and later, reeling home, he was telling everyone in earshot that 'my wifesh finest gurl in Shevvel!' Indeed, Jack was to discover in due course that his observation was completely accurate.

When he returned to work after the festivities, he was immediately pestered for the price of 'Wedding Ale', in other words—ten shillings. Now Jack, being a sensible chap, realised that now he was married, he couldn't afford to throw a half sovereign away, so he decided he had better ask his missis. For, even in the short time that they had been wed, Molly had become the 'Chancellor of the Exchequer' in their home.

A day or two later the newly married wife came proudly to the wheel, bringing her husband's dinner in a small wicker basket. 'Is t' mester in?' she asked, referring to her husband.

'He's not abaht, lass', shouted one of the men, who was known as Grinder Jim.

'Then I'll wait a bit—ah've brought his dinner' said Molly.

At this the grinders decided that here was an opportunity for a laugh at the newlywed's expense, so Grinder Jim retorted with a huge grin, 'Then if tha waits 'ere, thah'll 'ave to pay thi foot-ale!'

Thereupon the grinders gathered round the frightened girl, demanding ten shillings to drink her health. But the little woman was braver than they thought and she refused to pay.

Molly then found herself being seized by the half-dozen grinning workmen, who carried her like a baby to the drum board and plonked her down. Grinder Jim knelt down and clutched one of her feet.

'Tek 'er boot off, Jim!' shouted the grinders, thoroughly enjoying the woman's discomfiture.

Many horrible thoughts raced through Molly's head as she felt the men fumbling with her boot. What are the men going to do? Do they intend to denude me of all my clothing—to disrobe me until I stand before them like a cutlers' Lady Godiva? Never, I will die first! Oh, that my husband would come to my rescue!

Meanwhile Grinder Jim had seized her left ankle and his right hand clasped her boot heel. 'Will tha pay thi foot-ale?' he demanded savagely.

'No!' cried Molly, white with passion and struggling wildly. 'But here's mi foot!' And, striking out with her right leg, she sent her heel with sledge hammer force into the grinder's chest!

Backwards the big man went, rolling down the slanting floor like a human football. His fellow grinders were convulsed with glee, for the look of amazement on Grinder Jim's face was ludicrous to behold.

The chances are that if he had not been stopped by the door post, the man would have rolled down the bank into the River Sheaf. As it was his mouth and eyes were rimmed with wheel swarf, his face was bruised, his head cut and his chest as sore as if a horse had kicked him.

When the men turned from viewing the 'mighty fallen', they were just in time to see Molly stalking indignantly out of the grinding wheel. Not until she had disappeared did Jim get up to rub his bruises and to wipe the wheel swarf off his teeth. Then, amidst the scoffing of his mates, he went home, finally resolved that he would negotiate for foot-ale no more.

Just a year afterwards Molly presented her husband with a bouncing baby boy, but Jack Grindleblade was never asked for 'child's-ale', the ten shillings that was normally levied on a grinder when his first child was born!

The Jolly Grinder

From a street ballad printed by Joseph Ford.

There was a jolly grinder once,
Liv'd by the River Don;
He work'd and sang from morn to night,
And sometimes he'd work none!
But still the burden of his song,
For ever used to be—
Tis never worth while to work too long,
For it doesn't agree with me!

Mary Ann of Malin Bridge

During the time when water power was the main method of turning grinding wheels and working trip hammers, a local saying amongst the grinders and workers of the wheels on the River Loxley was 'Mary Ann has been in her pattens!'

This saying originated because of the habit of the grinders, who, during the week, would go for ale to a public house at Malin Bridge, kept by a woman called Mary Ann. They would ask for the ale consumed to be put on the slate, giving their promise to pay in full at the weekend.

If any of the wheels defaulted, Ann would go in the night to that particular wheel and remove the drive-belt that turned the grindstones. The wheel would not receive the drive-belt back until the previous week's debt had been paid.

Pattens were the wooden shoes or clogs worn at that time, hence the favourite saying when a drive belt was off or anyone's tools were missing—'Mary Ann has been in her pattens!'

The Strange Story of Benjamin Garside Elliott

Most Sheffield people will have heard of Ebenezer Elliott, the poet, he came to live in the town in 1821, made a fortune here, and because of his poems against the cruel Corn Laws, had a statue[3] erected to his memory in the Market Place.

However, few will know of the following story of the strange end of the eccentric Benjamin Garside Elliott, one of Ebenezer's sons.

Benjamin lived practically all his life in a little hamlet north of Sheffield called Shiregreen. His cottage presented a poor picture, always in a state of disrepair, the windows broken, with shutters usually kept closed, and a weed infested, neglected garden.

The interior of the cottage was to most people a mysterious unknown. Boys living in the village believed the place to be full of arms and weapons, a tale probably spread around after the milk boy had spotted a rusty gun when Benjamin had opened the door slightly to receive his milk.

Benjamin never let anyone enter his home and he seldom left it himself except for walks which he always took at the strange hour of midnight. Sometimes on these nocturnal ramblings he would meet the village policeman and they would walk along together. Because Benjamin always armed himself with a bill-hook and carried a pistol in his pocket, wild tales were circulated about him amongst the folk of Shiregreen and Wincobank.

However, in reality, the man was harmless and he would probably have been as amazed as anybody at the tales told about him.

One Sunday, in December, 1867, he confided to his friend the policeman that he was apprehensive of approaching death—and that was the last time he was seen alive!

The following day, which had been preceded by a very cold night, the milk boy received no response to his knock but, because of Benjamin's eccentricity, he took no notice at the time.

However, when the recluse failed to open the door again on the Tuesday, the milk boy went for help and the cottage door was forced open.

On the floor of the kitchen, in wonderful confusion, lay clothes, food, domestic utensils, weapons, books, newspapers and piles of miscellaneous lumber! Then by the sinkstone they saw the body of Benjamin, lying where he had collapsed, obviously early on Monday morning.

Though the mystery of the cottage had now been revealed, the villagers still had their misgivings about this house of death and a little crowd waited outside the door for the arrival of the authorities from Sheffield.

Examination of the contents of the cottage revealed that Benjamin had been no ordinary recluse. Various books and writings proved that he had possessed considerable power of mind, and that he had excellent taste in art was evinced by the fine paintings that adorned the walls and the quality and character of the furniture. By the couch, where he would recline and read, a well-worn copy of Mrs Shelley's *Frankenstein* was found.

What a pity it seems, that the son of such a noted poet, should at his end become a gazing stock for the local rustics and that all that could be said at the time was compressed into the laconic verdict of the coroner's jury—'Found dead!'

The Friendly Ghost of Bramley Hall

Situated in Bramley Hall Road, Handsworth, though now surrounded by a housing estate, is the fine building known as Bramley Hall. This hall is said to be haunted by a friendly ghost!

It appears that when the first hall on this site was occupied by Hugh de Bramley, a Norman lord who lived in the 13th century, a monk coming from Kirkstead Abbey in Lincolnshire, to Sheffield, was attacked by thieves and left lying badly injured in a hedgerow not far from Bramley Hall.

The following day servants of de Bramley discovered this unfortunate holy man and, upon their master's bequest, they carried him to the Hall. There he was given a bed and his wounds were attended to. However, the poor fellow had been hit upon the head many times, causing deep wounds and a considerable loss of blood, and this, together with the lack of medical knowledge at the time, caused his death the following day.

An ancient legend says that each year, on the anniversary of that foul murder, the monk returns to Bramley Hall to wander around the garden and rooms of the beautiful Georgian house that now occupies the site.

No one need be frightened of this ghost however, for because of the kind treatment bestowed upon him by Hugh de Bramley and his staff, the phantom monk wears a benevolent smile and holds out his hands in benediction should he be seen by any mortal being.

The Unfortunate John Unwin of Dore

In the early 19th century, there lived at Dore a man called John Unwin who, it seems, was a very keen inventor. One of his inventions was a diving bell, this was sent to Manchester to be tested and it proved to be very satisfactory.

Unfortunately, however, a workman in the Manchester factory, fascinated by the unusual machine, climbed inside when no one was about and lowered the bell into about twelve feet of water. Not being familiar with the controls, he must have used the wrong levers, for water rushed into the diving bell and he was instantly drowned.

This accident so enraged all the other workmen that they smashed the invention completely and they would also have done serious injury to John Unwin if they could have laid hands upon him.

This mishap ended, for ever, the Dore man's inventions for the diving world!

The Story of Betty and the Whatcake

One wet Monday morning in the 1800s, an old woman who lived just outside the village of Dore passed down the village street. She was obviously dressed in her best clothes, had pattens on her feet and she proudly carried her one and only umbrella.

The village schoolmistress happened to be standing at the door of the school, which was also her cottage, and she was extremely surprised to see Betty at such an unusual time. She called 'Betty, where are you going?'

'I'm for the chapel' answered Betty, surprised at being questioned.

'Ah, going to be married?' asked the schoolmistress, with a broad smile.

'Noo!' was Betty's response.

'What then?' was the next question.

'What do we go every Sunday for?' Betty asked.

A look of amazement came over the schoolteacher's face. 'Sunday! But it's Monday today!' she exclaimed.

'The ferrits it is!' grumbled Betty, realisation dawning. 'Then its the old whatcake (oatcake) what's done it!'

'But how's that?' asked the schoolmistress.

'Why' responded Betty, 'I always bake a peck of meal and it just serves me a week, but it happened to make two cakes more this time and that's driven me into Monday. What makes it worse' continued the old woman, apparently horrified at breaking the Sabbath, 'I was whitewashing yesterday!'

The Pleasures of Ballooning

In the late 19th century a favourite sport for the well-to-do adventurous person was ballooning. Many accounts are recorded of various ascents, but I think the following gives a perfect picture of the thrills and entertainment provided by the sport.

The balloon, which was the property of Spencers of London, was due to leave the Botanical Gardens just after one o'clock in the afternoon. The day was fine, with a clear sky and the wind seemed ideal for the ascent. Crowds of people had paid to enter the gardens to witness the daring aeronauts set forth on their journey.

A local man, Mr E. Parker Hydes, of Nether Edge, was the chief aeronaut and at 1.40 p.m. he decided that conditions were right for the take off. Upon his shout, the rope holders let go and the balloon started to drift away in a south-westerly direction. It then appeared that there was the possibility of a nasty accident, as some large poplar trees stood directly in the path of the rising balloon. Luckily a slight variation in the wind saved the aeronauts from disaster.

As the crowd cheered lustily, the balloon rose steadily and, as Mr Hydes remarked later 'What a pity that Sheffield should be enveloped in so much smoke, otherwise as we hung between Ranmoor and Ecclesall, we should have seen it from end to end!'

Though only in the air for ten minutes, the balloon had reached a height of 2,000 feet and people watching in Nether Edge, Heeley and Meersbrook, had an excellent view of the ascent.

The daring aeronauts then passed over Dore Station, leaving Ecclesall on the right. Now the balloon was at a height of 3,000 feet and passing over Totley, with miles of beautiful moorland country on the left and ahead. This made a glorious panorama, with Holmsfield Church and the Owler Bar Inn easily recognisable features. Keeping to the same height, the balloon passed over Chatsworth, the River Derwent and Rowsley.

As with most balloon flights, the landing was the most dangerous part of the trip, but luckily a good set down was made in a field near Hoon, about one mile from

Tutbury Station. The aeronauts then walked across the fields to a farmhouse where the farmer agreed to lend them a horse and cart to carry the collapsed balloon away.

The daring travellers then caught the six o'clock train to Derby Station where they had refreshments. Afterwards they left Derby on the 8 o'clock train and they returned to Sheffield after what they described as 'a most enjoyable day!'

An advertisement later inserted in the *Weekly Independent* of 1894, stated:

> *Anyone wanting to take a trip and view the wonders of nature, should contact Mr E. Parker Hydes, of Nether Edge, who will gladly arrange for an ascent upon a favourable day.*

An Early Aeronautical Engineer

One does not usually associate Sheffield with the invention of the aeroplane, but it is an interesting fact that one of Sheffield's sons had a part to play in the study of engine powered flight!

John Stringfellow, who was born at Attercliffe on December 6th, 1799, designed and constructed the first ever engine-driven model aeroplane to make a free flight.

John's father had also had a great interest in science and mechanics and he encouraged his son in his studies. The engines made for the model planes were steam driven and had the highest power–weight ratio of that time.

John Stringfellow died on December 13th, 1883, aged 84.

Double 'uns in Paradise Square

Without a doubt one of the most fascinating places in Sheffield is Paradise Square, a fine, cobbled open space surrounded by houses built in 1736 and 1771.

Originally a cornfield, it was leased in 1736 by Thomas Broadbent, who lived in the Old Banker's House, which is still standing in Hartshead. It was he who built most of the houses we see today.

An old poem gives an insight into the Paradise Square of ancient days:

> *You may form to your fancy a stile which once stood*
> *Near the little Grape Tavern and made up of wood;*
> *On the side of a field then belonging to Hicks,*
> *Where children at that time hav't oft gathered sticks,*
> *'Twas called 'Hicks Stile Field' and there corn was oft grown,*
> *But 'Paradise Row' since the stile was took down,*
> *Many years it continued with houses, one row,*
> *But now 'tis a beautiful square as you know,*
> *With a Freemasons' Lodge and a flight of stone stairs,*
> *And under it shops with various wares.*

One house in Paradise Square had a cellar kitchen where griddle cakes, oat cakes, pikelets and so on were made. A flight of steps leading from this kitchen had a half door at the top.

A lady who was a caretaker at the house, because she was getting old, engaged a 'strapping wench' from the country, to assist her with her work. Then, as to be expected, within weeks a local lad came a-courting and this was mostly carried on over the half door at the top of the steps.

One day the old lady remarked to a neighbour that she thought there would soon be a wedding judging by the kissing she heard. She then added 'I counted up to twenty, but when "double 'uns" started I lost count!'

How Heeley Duff'em Acquired its Name

The ancient village of Heeley, even today, is often referred to by the local folk as 'Heeley Duff'em' though few people now know how the nickname originated.

In olden times the little stream called the Meers Brook was the boundary between Yorkshire and Derbyshire. The path of the stream is through Meersbrook under the main Chesterfield Road (just above Albert Road) at Heeley, from where it flows into the River Sheaf at Saxon Bridge. Immediately over the culvert that carries the stream under Chesterfield Road, was the Heeley Toll Bar. Its position meant that when the toll gate was closed it was in Yorkshire, but when it was opened it was in Derbyshire. This led to the proud boast by the toll keeper that he had walked from Yorkshire into Derbyshire and back more times than any other man!

In the old days people were often sent to prison for debt, for very few working class people had any possessions worth selling to pay off their debt. As the Sheffield bailiffs had no jurisdiction in Derbyshire, a person could escape being sent to jail by simply crossing over the Meers Brook at Heeley.

As the area near the toll bar was the nearest to Derbyshire, it was generally assumed that folk going to live at Heeley were going there to 'duff' (i.e. not pay) their creditors.

Later, when the County Court Acts were passed giving Sheffield jurisdiction right into Derbyshire as far as Norton and Greenhill, it was then of no advantage to live at Heeley, but the nickname has stuck!

The Nosey Ecclesfield Folk

Letters to the editors of local newspapers often give an amusing and illuminating insight into the manners of the times and the following extract, from a letter to the *Weekly Independent* of 1875, amply illustrates this point.

> *From Southey the passer-by has a fine view of Walkley, than which there is no more creditable suburb of Sheffield. These odd cottages in their little garden plots speak*

volumes for the industry and thrift of the cutlers and grinders by whom they were mainly built. The district north of Wadsley Bridge, of which Ecclesfield is the centre, is peopled by, I grant, a good hearted, but most bad mannered race of people. Every woman at her doorstead, every group at the street corner, every straggler in the street make the stranger the centre of a stolid stare. Hereabouts everybody knows everybody else and their business, and the countenances of everybody seem to denote that the thoughts within are, 'Who's that?', 'Where's he going?', 'What's he doing?' and so forth!'

A Remarkable Suite of Furniture

Sheffield craftsmen have made many beautiful and exquisite works of art over the last three hundred years, but nothing can have been more remarkable than the suite of furniture made, in 1904, for an Indian Rajah by the firm of Mappin and Webb.

The furniture, constructed mostly of solid silver, comprised: a four poster bed, twelve dining room and easy chairs, two couches, four tables, a drawing room cabinet and a lady's dressing table.

The bedstead was eight feet long by six feet broad and thirteen feet six inches high. On it were beautiful panels depicting in relief allegorical representations of Sleep, after pictures painted by Albert Moore RA.

All the furniture was in Chippendale and French marquetry style. Light frames of oak were made for the chairs, upon which sterling silver was solidly fitted, with upholstery of rich Indian Silk brocade. The tables were entirely of solid silver!

As the price paid was never divulged, one can only guess at the cost of this wonderful silver suite.

A Willow Tree from Napoleon's Tomb

Just off the main Barnsley Road, at its junction with Norwood Road, lies the once sleepy little hamlet of Crabtree. Here can still be seen 'Rose Cottage' a delightful house built in the late seventeenth century. In the garden of Rose Cottage is a tree of unusual ancestry.

It appears that a willow tree was planted here in the early 1920s by Mrs Franklin, whose husband owned the cottage and who was manager of Handbridges of Fargate.

Before her marriage, for many years, Mrs Franklin had been a companion to a wealthy family who travelled around the world a great deal. A member of this family had taken a cutting from the willow tree that grows on Napoleon's tomb at St Helena and planted it on their return.

When Mrs Franklin married, she took a cutting from this tree and planted it in her garden. Later, when she came to live at Rose Cottage, she took a cutting from the third tree, this has now grown and flourishes at Crabtree.

The Bellman, the Lamplighter, the Baker and the Sweep

In the early nineteenth century advertising was done by the official Bellman, a fellow named Ward, who lived in Milk Street.

'Old Ward' as he was always called, had a smart uniform comprising a blue coat with red facings and bright buttons and he wore a tall hat with a broad gold band. He carried a large brass bell which he would ring loudly to attract attention, then 'cried' the advertisements, gave notice of public meetings, auctions or whatever, and also informed of lost children or articles.

Street lighting when gas lamps were first introduced was a rather primitive affair, it necessitated a man carrying a ladder which he had to climb at each lamp-post, so that he could light the gas with a match or small hand lamp.

The carrying of the ladders round some of the narrow streets of Sheffield caused quite a few incidents, such as the one that happened at the Norfolk Street end of George Street.

Turning the sharp corner, a lamplighter called Jim Elliott, inadvertently poked his ladder into the stomach of a man coming along George Street. At the same time as he swung the ladder round Jim called out 'Mind!' The poor chap who had suffered the blow, asked ruefully 'Why, Ar tha goin' to do it agean?'

Many antiquated methods were used by Sheffield tradesmen of those times, one of these being very evident at the bakehouse of 'Baker George' which was next to the Old Barleycorn public house in Coal Pitt Lane.

George had a long wooden trough fitted to the floor and in this he kneaded the dough by treading it in the same way as men used to tread clay for making steel melting pots.

With his trousers rolled up to his knees, the baker trod the dough with his bare feet and everyone acknowledged that without doubt Baker George produced the best bread in Sheffield!

Ted Mills was born in the vicinity of Broomhall Street in 1839 and, at the age of eight, he was apprenticed to a chimney sweep. In those days the method of cleaning a chimney was to send young boys equipped with a small brush up the chimney to dislodge the soot. This was collected in sacks for later sale to local farmers.

Ted had to climb the chimneys stark naked, he worked all day and for this he received the magnificent wage of two pence a week. His employer was very hard—'a bad man an' all 'e wor' Ted remarked later in life. As the sweep's wife kept a small shop, one condition of Ted's employment was that he spent all his tuppence there.

The boy was only once stuck in a chimney, but he was fast for two hours—a rather frightening experience. However, at one time he went up a public house chimney to rescue another sweep boy who was stuck and afterwards the grateful landlady gave Ted sixpence and a bottle of ginger beer. The young chimney sweep never felt so rich as he did on that day!

Ted often had to sweep the chimneys at the Town Hall, and because one of these chimneys had ten bends it made the cleaning a very difficult operation. One boy would work his way slowly to the top and he would send down the soot for another to catch in a sack. Sometimes Ted would sweep as many as thirty chimneys in a day.

Ted Mills carried on the trade all his life, he died in 1921 at the age of eighty-two. Neither he nor his wife could read or write—but both had great powers of mental arithmetic when it came to reckoning up the bills!

Dooleyism on the Victoria Railway Station

The old London and North Eastern Railway Station, at the end of the Wicker, was a maze of tunnels, lifts and bridges and these were put to a singular use in the 1920s by a porter named Dooley.

At that time the porter's wages were very low and these men relied upon tips to make a reasonable living. So that these tips were always forthcoming, Dooley would approach any hesitant travellers standing on one of the platforms and enquire which train they required. Upon being told it was the so-and-so train, Dooley would inform the passengers that they were on the wrong platform and, picking up their luggage, he would make the polite request 'Follow me please'.

The wily porter would then take them along the platform, down a lift, through a tunnel under the line, up some steps, along a platform, over a bridge and after a few minutes of puffing and walking, would deposit the travellers and their luggage on some other part of the platform from which they had originally started. Naturally the travellers would be greatly obliged to the helpful porter and a sixpenny tip would invariably be his reward.

This method of increasing their wages became very popular with some of the other porters at the old Victoria Station and the custom became known, after its founder, as 'Dooleyism'.

Some Quaint Customs of Ancient Days

A great event held in Sheffield, which survived right down to the year 1826, was the 'Summer Game'. It was not only a great attraction for the people, with its sports and games, but it was very profitable—especially in the year 1550.

At that time money was raised by the prodigious drinking of beer which was brewed in the church house and sold at a high price. This was the chief means of supporting three chaplains of the Parish Church.

In early times a lot of importance was attached to the twelve days of Christmas. People would watch the sky during the whole of the twelve days, because they believed that as the weather was each day, so would be the weather of each month of the new year. The watchers would take it in turns to sit up at night and on the last day they each had a large share of a great plum cake.

In 1609 the Court Leet[4] of Sheffield made a rule that nobody could walk or talk in the street from 9 o'clock in the evening till 3 o'clock in the morning, so as not to annoy honest men and householders. Anyone breaking this rule was fined ten shillings. The curfew bell rang at 9 p.m. when everyone went to bed and the day bell rang at 4 a.m. the time for getting up and commencing work!

By another rule of the Court Leet, it was ordered that no person should make any wedding dinner for which he should take above sixpence a person and the penalty for so doing was £1 for each offence. It was the custom in those days for the bridegroom to take the bride to his house immediately after the wedding and give a series of feasts extending over ten days or a fortnight. At these feasts the guests had to pay and the charge was such as to yield a considerable profit for the newly married pair and this money often set them up for a number of years.

The Legend of Ringinglow[5]

On a certain Tuesday evening in the winter of a year in the eighteenth century, a Sheffield man lost his way when crossing the moors. The poor man tried for a long time to regain the path, but eventually he gave up in despair.

Suddenly he heard, very faintly in the distance, the sound of the bells of Sheffield Parish Church and following the direction of the sound, the traveller at last arrived safely home.

Feeling that the ringers of the bells had in all probability been the means of saving him from perishing on the bleak moors, he gave a sum of money to be divided among the ringers on that same night every year.

Because the Parish Church bells had been heard 'ringing low', from that time onwards that particular stretch of moorland was given the name it bears today.

Murder at Ringinglow

In April, 1876, quite a stir was created by a hoax concocted by a couple of rival journalists.

In order to boost sales of his newspaper, the first journalist put out a placard in town which read 'Horrid Murder in Ringinglow'. Not to be outdone a rival issued a similar placard bearing the legend 'Body Found!'

These announcements caused scores of people to walk to Ringinglow to see what they could see and, naturally, after wandering about for hours and finding no trace of the murder, they finished up at the Norfolk Arms.

The landlord of that establishment was called Garrett and he did a roaring trade out of the weary travellers. Were the journalists and the landlord in league? If so, it never came to light!

The Exhausted Cricketers

In the early nineteenth century the top of Carver Street marked the limit of Sheffield. Where Carver Street Chapel now stands was a large piece of ground called Hutton Field. This field was the principal cricket ground for the neighbourhood and many excellent matches were played there.

At one of these matches there was a player called Orsgethorpe who proved without doubt to be the best batsman of the day. He either hit or blocked every ball and though the bowlers tried every way to get him out, right through the whole day, they were unsuccessful. Eventually they were so tired they all lay down on the field in despair! Needless to say Orsgethorpe's side won the match.

The Giant Pioneer

Past the top of Carver Street all was open country to the west. At Trippet Lane the Grapes Public House was the end of Sheffield in that direction. Where Portobello Street now is, there was a long narrow lane, more like a gutter, with a high hedge on each side. Broad Lane finished at about what was to become the site of St George's churchyard and all was fields and gardens beyond except for, here and there, a gentleman's house.

Near the top of Trippet Lane lived a man called Curtis. He was very tall, being six feet two inches in height, was well built and very erect.

Naturally, he entered the army, as a volunteer in the Old Sheffield Blues at the latter end of the 1700s. When the commander saw the new recruit he was struck by his size and bearing, so he was immediately made a Pioneer. He was then issued with a tall grenadier head-dress that made him seem seven feet high and he was given a large hatchet to carry.

When on parade through the streets of Sheffield, Curtis led the regiment, looking, as one can imagine, a very formidable sight!

Post Office Cows

Towards the end of the 18th century when the Post Office was in Orchard Street, mail-coach drivers and the inhabitants complained about the office being in such a narrow street, with so many sharp corners. The excuse made by the Postmaster for wanting that particular site was that he was able to keep his cows in the fields at the rear of his premises. However, his successor, abiding by the wishes of the townspeople, opened a new post office at the corner of Arundel Street and Norfolk Street.

Climbing the Church Spire

The repair of church steeples used to be carried out by a journeyman builder who used the method of nailing ladders against the side of the steeple, much quicker and cheaper than using scaffolding.

A builder was engaged to repair the Sheffield Parish Church spire and he commenced by nailing ladders right to the top of the steeple so that he could then do the repair work with ease. While this work was going on, William Batty came on the scene. Everyone in Sheffield knew that Batty never refused a dare and so he was challenged to climb to the top of the spire.

Batty not only climbed the steeple, but when he reached the top he played a tune on a French horn—much to the amusement of the crowd watching from below.

When Time Stood Still

Reliance in bygone days on the chiming of the Parish Church clock for telling the time, once saved a woman from spending a most uncomfortable night.

Martha Wright was a singer at the church and on this particular occasion, the sermon being rather dull, she had fallen asleep in one of the rear pews. When she awoke she found everyone had gone and that she was locked in the church. She tried in vain to make herself heard, then suddenly she had an idea. Going into the clock tower, she arrested the swing of the large pendulum, thereby stopping the clock and the chimes. The absence of the usual indications of the passing of time soon attracted the attention of people round about and upon investigation the woman was released.

The Legend of the Executioner

About the year 1700, a venerable old man called William Walker, came to reside in the village of Darnall.

Walker turned out to be a man of wisdom, spending most of his time with books. He must also have had leanings towards astronomy for he was fond of gazing into the night sky, an occupation that caused some suspicion among the local people. This suspicion was augmented by Walker's lack of communication, for Walker kept himself very much to himself and refused to be drawn into lengthy conversation.

Such a man, human nature being what it is, was soon the object of dislike by the rustic population. The story then spread around that William Walker was the same Walker who had cut off the head of King Charles I and that, fearing for his safety after the Restoration, he had fled from the Court to wander about the land until he eventually settled at Darnall. Once this rumour was started, nothing could stop it and even after the Cutlers' Company bestowed upon him the honorary freedom of their association, this never prevented the local people pointing out William Walker as the 'dreaded executioner'.

The Old Sheffield Volunteers

To be in the Volunteers a working man had to sacrifice a great deal, for he lost a week's wages when in camp. The Hallamshire headquarters was situated in Eyre Street. The men drilled in civilian clothes and made a brave show marching down Matilda Street with the band in front.

The Artillery Volunteers had their headquarters in Tudor Street, where the Lyceum Theatre is today. These men were very proud of their small, round pillbox hats.

The Yeomanry had both large and small horses and the men wore a helmet similar in style to that of the Life Guards. Their headquarters was in Norfolk Street. Some of the horses used by the Yeomanry were used for drawing milk carts during the week and so, when the volunteers were parading through the town, some wag would shout 'Milk!' and all the milk horses would stop dead, throwing the ranks into utter confusion!

Agony Column

The study of nineteenth century newspapers produces much that is enlightening and amusing, as, for example, this advertisement published in the *Sheffield Mercury* of April, 1833.

> *An advertisement appeared a few days ago concerning a young lady who had eloped. She is most earnestly requested to return to her disconsolate parents; but, if she will not return, she is earnestly desired to send the key to the tea chest.*

There is no record of the result of this heart-rending appeal!

Gallant Captain Bess

'Captain Bess' was the title given by the folk in the Sheffield area, to Elizabeth Birley of Middlewood House, who married William Longsdon, a member of an old Derbyshire family.

It appears that during a skirmish near Sheffield in the Civil War, Captain Longsdon was seriously wounded. As often happened in those days, his wife, who was large with child, was amongst the spectators watching the battle. Being on horseback, Elizabeth, at great danger to herself, rode into the fray and rescued her husband. Then, leaving him with some friends, the gallant lady returned to the field of battle and assumed command of her husband's men. Her wonderful bravery on this day earned her the title of 'Captain Bess'. After the battle Elizabeth had her husband carried to Middlewood House, where, despite her tender care, he died of his wounds. Captain Longsdon was buried under the east window of the Sheffield Parish Church and, within a few days of this sad event, Captain Bess gave birth to a son.

A Legend of Loxley Common

It was a bitterly cold day in the year 1812, the sun had set early and low storm clouds hung over Loxley Common.

In a lonely cottage on the bleak moorland, a mother crooned over her sleeping baby, meanwhile listening for the sound of her husband's footsteps. Lomas Revill, gamekeeper to the Lord of the Manor, was late and for his wife it was a weary vigil, relieved only by the visit of a woman friend from one of the cottages on the hillside.

When she had gone Mary Revill watched the flickering uncanny shadows cast by the log fire, until eventually, weariness overtaking her, she nodded off to sleep.

Struggling fitfully the moon sought to pierce the heavy snow clouds, but with little success, and the wind howled across the common. As the hours passed the storm mounted in intensity and blinding snow swept the landscape until it was shrouded in a thick mantle of white.

The following day was New Year's Eve and, as morning broke cold but fine, an acquaintance from the adjacent hamlet of Wadsley called to exchange the compliments of the day with the dwellers in the lonely cottage. The visitor knocked again and again, but getting no response she tried the latch and finding the door would open, she entered the room.

A horrible sight met her eyes! Poor Mary Revill lay on the floor in a pool of blood—murdered! Whilst in the cradle near the body the baby lay fast asleep. Outside the cottage the world was clad in white. During the night the snow had drifted all along the heath and piled itself upon the crags which formed a rough boundary between Loxley Common and Wadsley Common.

Leading from the cottage and right across the ridge and over the open common were large footprints, some partly obliterated by the drifting snow, but all leading in one direction, to a cave-like well on the crown of the hill overlooking the valley. The footprints went distinctly to the cave, into it and disappeared. Strangest of all, as far as could be discerned, there were no footprints leading out of the cave.

When the news of this terrible crime spread around the neighbouring hamlets, there was much weird speculation. Who was the murderer? What was the mystery of the footprints to the cave?

Meanwhile Lomas Revill had been found in the gamekeepers' cabin far out in the woods. When told of the tragic death of his wife he accepted the news with little show of surprise or emotion. Though he had been seen in the village inn, much the worse for drink, on the night of the tragedy, no one could swear that the gamekeeper hadn't spent the night in his cabin.

The moorland murder remained a mystery and for years the good folk of the area fought shy of being anywhere near the Loxley cave after night had fallen.

As time went by, Lomas Revill became a strange man, and prematurely aged with white hair, even though he was only 42 years old.

Another New Year's Eve came and once more the common was deep in snow. At the local inn someone remarked that he hadn't seen the gamekeeper for a number of days so, deciding to investigate, a number of men made up a party and went along to the cabin in the woods.

No trace being found of Lomas, they then tramped over the common to the old cottage, and there, in an outbuilding, they found his body hanging from a rafter!

Later a search of the cabin in the woods revealed a hunter's knife rusted in gore, and a pair of blood-stained gaiters. Folk who had known Lomas Revill well, said that he had always acted strangely when New Year's Eve came round and that he had often been heard to mutter that he couldn't stand life any longer.

Beyond this, and the articles found in the cabin, there was nothing to connect the gamekeeper with the murder of his wife. However, superstition had seized the simple, homely people of the countryside and when storm clouds frowned, when snow whistled in the wind over the common, and pale moonlight cast its haunting shadows on crag and heath, 'tis said the ghost of Mary Revill walked abroad.

Wanderers over the common and the lanes about, thought of Frank Fern's gibbet,[6] creaking in the wind on the Edge only a stone's throw away and all but the stout hearted feared to pass that way at night lest they should hear the clanking of Frank Fern's chains or encounter the ghost of that poor unfortunate mother. For many years afterwards a number of cottages stood empty, falling into ruin, because of the common's association with the murder of Mary Revill.

A Walk from Sheffield to Beauchief in the Early Nineteenth Century

Based on fact and written in the style of that period

It was about noon on a delightful September day, when we departed from the King's Head[7] in Change Alley, to walk to Beauchief. My companions, Mr and Mrs Williams, relatives of my late dear wife, were in the course of spending a few days in Sheffield and I had promised to escort them, during their short stay, to see some of the countryside which is adjacent to our small town.

After bidding farewell to mine host, we passed along the busy High Street, Fargate and Pinstone Lane, then turned down Union Street, where my guests greatly admired the fine erections now being built in that area.

Leaving the town, we proceeded down South Street, as the road down the Sheffield moor is called, passing on our right the old Angel Inn,[8] and noticing as we walked down the road, that many houses are now in the course of erection.

Crossing the bridge over the Porter Brook,[9] at the bottom of South Street, I pointed out to Mr and Mrs Williams the Saw Mill, where in the evenings, two men are usually available to escort persons on foot along the footpath to Sharrow Head. This, of course, is necessary owing to the number of footpads which lurk in this area, ready to pounce on some tired and unsuspecting traveller.

On the left, just before reaching Little Sheffield, we admired the pretty cottage[10] with the large pear tree in the front garden. I informed my friends that this latter, when full of fruit, is a great source of temptation to the neighbouring youths.

After walking through Little Sheffield past many little cottages, we proceeded along Broomfield,[11] where we found to our dismay, that all the country towards High Field, had been staked out for allotments, probably later to be sold for building. There are, at the present time, only a few cottages in this vicinity.

Reaching the High Field, my friends remarked upon the large expanse of meadow there and Mrs Williams was charmed by the large residence of Mount Pleasant[12] near the bottom of Sharrow Lane. A few yards further on we found a cottage set in a delightful garden, where we could rest and take refreshment, meanwhile feasting our eyes on the prospect before us. Just below the garden gate, the road on which we had travelled from town divided, the right hand branch leading by Totley and Dore to Bakewell and the left to Chesterfield by way of Heeley.

We decided that after taking our rest we should take the latter road and this we did, passing on the right the Low Field and its farmhouse, arriving shortly at Heeley Bridge. Pausing on the old bridge, which was first erected in 1567, we watched the little Sheaf, a pleasant river that, owing to the lack of rain during the preceding month, was running very low. I warned my friends not to be deceived by this trickle of water, as I had many times seen the Sheaf in flood and much damage has been caused when it has overflowed its banks.

However, time was passing and we still had much to see, so continuing our perambulations, we walked onwards and found ourselves in Derbyshire. By a large water-wheel called Heeley Mill,[13] we turned right and entered a field path and now indeed began to feel amongst the beauties of our ramble. This pathway, following the river, next led us past the Little London Tilt[14] and then winding round, it brought us to what is locally called Smithy Wood Bottom. Here were no less than three water-wheels at the side of a large expanse of water and

Mr Williams remarked on the ponderous movements of the ancient grinding machinery.

The vicinity of this dam is noted for its beauty and on this fine autumnal day, with the sun breaking through the light fleecy clouds, all the scenery around us was broken into the softest masses, making our feelings calm and serene, harmonising them with earth and sky.

Looking down the Abbey Dale we counted many shades of green, with here and there, the roofs of some fine houses just to be seen amongst the trees. A little further along this delightful pathway, I pointed out to my companions the little St Anne's (or Anna's) Well,[15] and whilst we refreshed ourselves with a drink of the sparkling, cold water, I told them, in verse, the legend of this small well:

Anna's Well

The Vale of Beauchief is a pleasant vale!
And interjacent miles of loveliest scenery,
Betwixt our good old town and that sweet spot,
Repay a summer wanderer for his walk.
Reader, hast thou ne'er pass'd by Heeley Mill,
Along the cool dam side, and onward still
By the deep bottom of Smithy Wood?

Yea, surely so,—if, to delight thine eye,
Sweet walk or lovely prospect may avail,
Or sounds can charm thine ear.

Then would'st thou mark,
Beside the path, that runs embower'd along
The margin of the wood—a little well,
Transparent, and unrippled by its spring,
The water shines beneath its brink scoop'd circular.

The Redbreast and the Blackbird slake them here,
Winter, and Summer, and throughout the year.

Know then, kind reader, on a poet's word,
That this is Anna's Well: nor let the name
Displease thy fancy, nor offend thine ear,
As by my sole arbitrament imposed;
Nor think that rites, and ceremonial due,
Were here neglected when the name was given.

The lovely maid, in voluntary act,
Lav'd her white palms, and sipped the water here,
The water, as in token of assent
Enshrined her image in its bosom bright;

And when the woods were questioned of their will,
'Say, shall this well be Anna's? To my words
Echo, as sponsor, thrice responded "Anna's".'

And I would fain; that here each rambling girl
Should pause awhile; and the bird nesting youth
Forego his search—and to their jovial fellows
Point out this spot, and as they pass it, say,
There's Anna's Well!

Mrs Williams showed extreme delight at this charming story and she asked if I would later write down the poem for her, so that after she and her husband returned home, she could read and remember this pleasant interlude.

This I promised to do and continuing our walk, within a few minutes, we arrived at Norton Hammer[16]—as the tilt at that place is designated. Here, from the road that passes by, we saw the sweetest prospect imaginable, a vista of perspective to the westward of us that included a most interesting view of Banner Cross. The light fretted turrets rose from amongst the trees, while nearby we could see the roof and belfry of the adjacent Ecclesall Chapel. We then proceeded up the hill beyond and after a strenuous climb reached the summit, where we rested, meanwhile turning about to view the scenery we had just left. Now, from this height, we could see the tower of St George's Church rising gracefully in the distance, this being backed by the magnificently wooded hill of Wincobank, while nearer our imaginations rested on the spot:

Where, mid hill and dale and wood,
Sheffield in the valley stood.

Our walk at length brought us to Woodseats, where, on turning right up a narrow lane,[17] we passed a picturesque old farmhouse.

About half a mile further on the Chesterfield road I was able to point out to Mr and Mrs Williams, the little cottage where, very recently, Peter Raeney[18] had died. Peter, I explained to my friends, was a young man who was driven insane because his girl, Mary Jones, married another man in Sheffield on the very day she had promised to marry Peter at Dronfield Church. The shock to the poor young man was so great and his heart was so troubled, that he immediately took to his bed, which was situated in the rafters of this little cottage. There he stayed, in that cramped space, his legs doubled up under his chin, refusing to leave his bed, until his poor body became malformed and it was impossible for him to straighten out. Eventually, in this sorry state, he died.

My story of this poor man visibly affected Mrs Williams and I discreetly looked away as she wiped tears from her eyes. I therefore hastened to speak of something more cheerful and the opportunity arose, when a little further on we saw, again on our right hand side, the farmhouse of Jonathon Booth.[19]

In this ancient farmhouse, I explained to my companions, had lived Jonathon Booth, a gentleman who had a daughter who was ill in an uncommon manner, in the fact that she had fits of alternative raving, praying, ecstasy and moping. These fits troubled the poor girl for many years until, miraculously, they completely ceased. On the 5th of June, 1753, Wesley, the noted preacher, travelling through Sheffield, heard about this interesting phenomenon and he visited this old farmhouse and spoke to the girl and her father. Later, he preached a sermon here to a gathering of the Woodseats people. This story of such a wonderful cure considerably cheered Mrs Williams and banished the horror of the former tale from her mind. We then continued with our perambulations and turning right off the Chesterfield road, we entered Beauchief Lane.[20]

How far this lane may be fordable in winter, I know not; but even in this season, we found it in a miry state. It seemed the lane had been suffered to remain unmolested in its original foundation, ever since it was perambulated by the monks of Beauchief, to view their estates at 'Wodesetes'.

After traversing this lane for about a mile, we arrived at the Abbey, a building rather more venerable in association with its history in other days, than imposing in its present appearance. We rambled about with peculiar emotions amidst the few remaining fragments of this once considerable monastic pile and I remarked that the monastery had mostly perished, as the works of men are continually doing.

But, I exclaimed, amidst assent from Mr Williams and his dear wife, the hills remain, the River Sheaf runs merrily through the meadows and the green fields and wooded eminences still attest the wondrous beauty of Beauchief and the Abbey Dale.[21]

A Story of Old Sheffield

Based on an article published by Leader and Sons in 1866

Michael Lee was the master of a tool works that occupied a site on a croft near Castle Hill, now entirely covered by the large modern Castle Market. Master Lee, as he was known to his employees, had a son, Godfrey, and a daughter, Judith. The Lee family were very reserved, in fact the old man, Michael, who it is said had a hideous face, was intensely disliked by all the Sheffield people who knew him. Judith, though an unusually tall and handsome girl, seemed to have the same temperament as her father, but Godfrey was of a different character, pleasant and willing to help whom he could.

Strange stories were told amongst the townsfolk about Master Lee's tool works, how none of the tools, mostly agricultural, had names, just numbers; how these tools were loaded on to pack horses which left at night and, travelling by the light of the moon, made for a seaport on the west coast. How, ten days or so later, the pack horses returned, carrying casks which contained sugar and other foreign produce, to be sold later at Sheffield Market.

Children, though frightened of Master Lee, would, out of sheer bravado, climb the walls of the tool works in the evening and knock nails into the casks, hoping to make a hole big enough to allow the contents to escape. One particular evening, one of the casks broke open and the horrified children saw protruding through the gap, a black hand and arm.

Running home they fetched their parents who, upon investigation, found the contents of the cask to be a Negro, who judging by the marks upon his body, had been cruelly flogged to death.

The word went round the town like wildfire, obviously the tools made at Master Lee's were for the slave plantations of America, and the anger of the people grew to alarming proportions. That evening a large mob stormed the works, breaking the gates, sheds, and every other object they found within reach of their hammers and axes. Then, all the tools and anything portable were picked up and dumped in the River Don and Master Lee's works, as such, ceased to exist. The following day the Lee family left Sheffield and went to live in an isolated farm cottage on the moors near Dore. Here, except for the servants and an occasional farmer, the family saw no one and Master Lee and Judith became more withdrawn than ever.

Godfrey however, could not bear living on the wild moorlands and he eventually persuaded his father to allow him to live at Abbeydale and work a mill, one which had been in use since the time when it ground corn for the monks at Beauchief Abbey.

One day Godfrey was on his way to Sheffield town, via the old pack horse road from Abbeydale, which passed along what is now Kenwood and came out in Sharrow Lane and so down to town. Turning through the trees into Sharrow Lane, Godfrey saw a pretty teenage girl being assaulted by three youths and he instantly ran to her rescue. Being quite a well-built and strong young man, Godfrey soon had the upper hand and within minutes all three youths were lying in the ditch.

Escorting the girl to town, Godfrey discovered her name was Patience Westdale, and that her father was Obadiah Westdale, a Puritan stalwart of Sheffield. This gentleman was very proud of the fact that his great grandfather had fought alongside Colonel Bright, of Carbrook Hall, in the Civil Wars.

To Godfrey and Patience it was love at first sight, but when Godfrey asked Obadiah if he could pay court to his daughter, he was met with an instant rebuff and Patience was forbidden to see the young man again.

Meanwhile, the year being 1745, the Young Pretender, Charles Edward, had landed in Scotland and this crisis caused the country to be scoured for soldiers. This brought into the area an officer called Captain Monkton who, passing the Lee homestead at Dore, called at the farmhouse and demanded food for himself and his troops. Captain Monkton, who always had an eye for the ladies, was struck by the proud handsome beauty of Judith Lee and in the short time he was at the farm cottage he seduced the girl, promising his hand in marriage after the rebellion was over.

For Godfrey and Patience the days and weeks passed slowly. Each Sunday Godfrey would go to Nether Chapel just to get a glimpse of Patience sitting with her father, but of course, they were not allowed to speak a word.

Eventually, however, Godfrey managed to get a message to his sweetheart and sometimes they managed to meet in the grove of oaks that surrounded Broomhall Spring.[22] This little wooded beauty spot was situated where Wilkinson Street and Gell Street are today. The pair were so much in love that Godfrey again decided to brave the wrath of Patience's father, but old Obadiah was adamant, refusing to let them marry and telling Godfrey that he must not attempt to see his daughter again.

In December of that year, Prince Charles Edward began his retreat from Derby and Captain Monkton found himself attached to the small army of retreating Scots. Calling again on Judith Lee, the gallant captain realised he had now little interest in the girl, he left almost immediately but promising to return as soon as possible. Did Judith suspect that her soldier was deserting her? We can only guess.

However, three days after Captain Monkton had departed, servants at the Lee household, whilst going to fetch water from the pond near the house, stumbled upon the body of old Michael Lee lying partly covered by the snow that was still falling, the body was a grisly sight.

The servants immediately aroused Godfrey and Judith and, as both had appeared to be sleeping soundly, it appeared that Michael had been attacked by someone, perhaps a footpad, prowling about near the farm cottage. Godfrey despatched a servant to Sheffield to fetch a Minister of Justice, but before this worthy person arrived, a party of soldiers passing by called at the cottage and, when told of the crime that had been committed, they decided to investigate. The officer in charge of the troop examined the body and found a number of stab wounds, obviously caused by blows from a sharp knife. He also discovered indistinct footmarks in the snow leading back to the cottage. The officer ordered his men to search the house and in Godfrey's room, a blood stained clasp knife was found, also damp and muddy boots splashed with blood. Upon Godfrey's admission that these articles were his, he was immediately taken prisoner and charged with the murder of his father.

While awaiting to be tried at Derby Assizes, Godfrey was kept at Hathersage Hall and here Patience and her father were allowed to visit him. Old Obadiah, though still strong in his dislike of the Lee family, could not believe that Godfrey was guilty of the crime of murder and promised his daughter he would do all in his power to help the young man.

When the trial at Derby took place, everything seemed against Godfrey, all the evidence pointing to his guilt. To make matters worse, when Judith was called to give evidence for the defence, she swooned and did not revive sufficiently to be able to make any cohesive statement. Needless to say, Godfrey was found guilty and sentenced to the gallows.

After the trial Judith returned to Dore, hoping to find a letter from her lover, but neither letter nor the gallant captain were at the cottage. The angry Judith saddled her horse and set out to find Captain Monkton. Eventually, she caught up with him at Carlisle. Monkton was having a meal with fellow officers when a message was handed to him informing him of Judith's arrival. He sent a reply that he had no wish to see her again, but Judith forced her way into the room and, accusing him of playing her false, she informed him she was going to her doom and that she would take him with her! With this ominous threat and hatred in her heart, Judith returned to Dore vowing to get her revenge on the unfaithful Captain Monkton.

Meanwhile, in the condemned cell at Derby prison, old Obadiah Westdale was saying goodbye to Godfrey, regretting that his efforts to help him had been in vain. Patience was at their lodgings in Derby, too overwrought to set foot outside the house.

On the day set for the hanging, crowds began to gather even before dawn, all in eager anticipation of an entertaining spectacle. From all directions people poured into the area surrounding the gallows, all anxious to witness the last few minutes of the murderer of Michael Lee. However, when mid-day arrived and there was still no sign of the prisoner being brought from the gaol, angry mutterings arose from the mob, then grew in violence when they heard that Godfrey had escaped from the condemned cell and there would be no public hanging that day.

Two days later a wandering packman, or pedlar, arrived at the lodgings of the Westdales. The joy of Patience can only be imagined when the packman turned out to be none other than Godfrey Lee. To Patience and her father, Godfrey explained how, with the help of a friendly warder who believed in his innocence, he had escaped from Derby Gaol. How he had taken to the disguise of a packman, selling small wares, to wander about the streets of the town until he had discovered where the Westdales were lodging. He informed Patience she had no need to worry about him as he had found a good hiding place where he would be safe until he could prove his innocence.

After Godfrey had left, the Westdales returned to Sheffield, now much lighter in heart and hoping they would be able to discover evidence that would clear Godfrey's name.

This evidence was to come much sooner than they expected, for Judith Lee, her soul now twisted with hate, decided to get her revenge on Monkton by giving herself up and denouncing the Captain as the plotter and instigator of the murder of her father. Going to the Constable's Office she wrote out a full confession, stating that her brother Godfrey had tried to stop her relationship with Captain Monkton and, to bring about her brother's ruin, she and Monkton arranged to murder her father, the blame to fall upon Godfrey. She also produced a letter supposedly from Monkton incriminating himself in the plot.

Later, however, at the trial of Judith Lee, the letter was proved to be a forgery and the packed court listened with horror to Judith's confession of how she killed her father, stabbing him many times with Godfrey's clasp knife.

Judith, no longer the proud, handsome girl of former years, was sentenced to death and upon the day of the execution, a greater crowd than ever assembled round the gallows. As Judith mounted the scaffold, the sky darkened and a fierce thunderstorm broke out, thunder and lightning following in quick succession. It grew so dark that the small group of people on the gallows platform could only be seen during the brief flashes of lightning and the crowd grew silent as the hangman adjusted the rope. Suddenly, a terrific flash, greater than any which had gone before, lit up the awful scene and the mob gasped to see what appeared to be the disappearance of the victim before their eyes. Then, with the next flash, they saw the hangman bending over a burnt bundle of clothing. All that was left of Judith Lee was a scorched, blackened corpse!

The great mob of people, that had arrived anticipating an entertaining spectacle, dispersed in terror, hurrying to their homes horrified at the awful intervention of God.

The story ends on a happier note, for Godfrey Lee received a free pardon and, returning to Dore, he lived for a time in the cottage on the moors. Later he took up residence in the mill at Abbeydale and once again he visited Obadiah Westdale to ask for his daughter's hand. Again the old man refused, but Patience, on her knees, eventually persuaded her father that her only happiness lay in marrying Godfrey, and Obadiah gave his blessing.

The couple would have liked to have been married at Nether Chapel, but the law at that time still required that Nonconformists and Conformists alike should go to the Mother Church to be married. So they were married at the Parish Church, now the Anglican Cathedral, and enjoyed many happy years of life together.

Ancient Epitaphs

The practice, very prevalent today, of 'tidying up' our churchyards has robbed us of many interesting and amusing epitaphs which were common on gravestones in former times. The following brief selection are examples that existed in the churchyards of Sheffield.

In the Parish Churchyard a stone in memory of Richard Walker, of the Royal Regiment of Horse Guards, who died on June 22nd, 1800, stated:

Within this dark and silent grave
Here lies a soldier just and brave;
And when the awful trump shall sound
He is for settled quarters bound.

In the same churchyard, on the stone of Sarah Oliver, who died in 1818, aged 30, was an epitaph that could be read two ways:

She was—
But words are wanting to say what,
Think what a wife should be—
She was that!

Not an epitaph, but a pathetic inscription was found on a stone:

To the Memory of Aaron Nichells who departed this life, April 20th, 1810. Aged 63 years. Also Catherine, his wife, who departed this life on the same day. Aged 63.

The bursting of grinding wheels cost many lives in the grinding hulls of old Sheffield and an incident of this type caused the death of William Hobson in 1815. His gravestone bore the epitaph:

Beneath this stone a grinder lies,
A sudden death ath close his eyes;
He lost his life by the breaking of a stone,
We hope his soul to Heaven has gone.

In Beauchief Abbey Churchyard a stone of 1758 tells of a gamekeeper who accidentally shot himself:

A Game keeper I was at Beauchief Hall,
At Dore my fatal gun caused me to fall,
Which made a speedy passage through my head
And sent me to the mansions of the dead.
Repent in time, consider mortal man,
Thy race extends no further than a span,
Man is like a flower that's in the morning blown,
Then before the night, is withered and cut down.

Another stone in the same churchyard, dated 1801, has the inscription:

She was a wife loving and kind,
And to her husband always bore a virtuous mind
Even unto the very last,
I hope to the Lord, in heaven she's cast.

Finally, on a stone to the memory of John Kidd, who died in 1846 and was burried in St Philip's Churchyard:

Here lieth the body of John Kidd,
In eternal realms his soul is hid.
A railway engine did him kill
And crushed his poor head so ill.

Humour in Sheffield History

The lighter side of local history is illustrated in the following anecdotes which came to light during my researches into Sheffield life in 18th and 19th centuries.

The Lepping Stones and the Parson

The Lepping Stones across the River Don occupied a line about thirty yards below the Crescent Bridge, near the entrance to what is now the Wednesday Football Club. Pedestrians wishing to cross the river found it necessary to leap from stone to stone, whilst horse drawn vehicles forded the river on the Middlewood side.

The stepping stones were usually very greasy and many people, attempting to reach the other bank, fell in the water and got a soaking. One of these unfortunate persons was the Reverend Samuel Danks Waddy, who, on his way to preach at Wadsley Bridge Chapel, slipped and fell in the river while crossing the Lepping Stones—it is reported the good parson did not preach a 'dry' sermon on that particular day!

The Doctor and the Parson

One of the most unusual residents at Loxley House was a man called Henry Payne. A rather eccentric medical practitioner, his cure for all the ills of the flesh was simply a very hot blanket!

During the latter part of his life, Doctor Payne quarrelled with the parson in Wadsley. The outcome was that Payne swore he would never enter the church again. The parson insisted that he would, clinching his argument with the remark 'You will, when you are carried in head first in your coffin!'

However, the doctor was not to be defeated even in death, for he left orders that he was to be buried on his own estate without a church ceremony. So when he died, in 1895, two servants carried the coffin to a grave dug in the grounds of Loxley House, lowered the coffin in, and without any kind of religious ceremony, filled in the grave.

Disturbance in the Parish Church

Francis Jessop, Rector of Treeton, the younger son of Francis Jessop of Broom Hall, was one Sunday in the Parish Church listening to a sermon given by the Vicar, a Mr Drake.

Jessop, disagreeing with something the Vicar said, suddenly jumped up from his seat, levelled a loaded pistol at Mr Drake and shouted, 'Duck or Drake, I'll have at thee, mallard!'

He would actually have fired at the Vicar if he had not been restrained by his friends. Meanwhile, Mr Drake had crouched down behind his pulpit and he stayed trembling below until he was informed that Mr Jessop had been taken from the church!

The First Umbrella

Many amusing comments were made about the first people to carry umbrellas in the city.

The honour of being the first person to use such a device has been claimed for at least four people, these being: Mr Holy of Holy Green, Mr Greaves, Mr Newbould and William Trickett.

The latter was Master Cutler in 1771, and when he first appeared carrying an umbrella, his brother Enoch joined in the general laughter with the remark 'Si thi, our Bill's getten a walkin' stick wi' petticoats on!'

Duck Power

In 1854 a man called Harvey Teesdale floated down the River Don from West Bar in a basket pulled along by a number of ducks!

Horse Power

Up to 1911 a one-horse bus ran from Dore and Totley Station to Totley. It was driven by a little old man called Jimmy Larder. The nearest Jimmy had ever been to Sheffield was once when he visited Millhouses.

It is said that he used to shout and crack his whip loudly, but the old horse just ignored him and trotted on at its own slow pace!

Lucy the Pig

Situated in West Bar, near the corner of Corporation Street, was the Gaiety Music Hall, run by a German called Metzler. This gentleman had also a pork shop and a public house nearby.

Mr Metzler had a tame pig called Lucy that was very fond of beer. A customer gave it two quarts one day and the pig went under a table and lay very still.

Mr Metzler came in, looked at it and in a tone of disgust said 'Lucy's as drunk as a pig!'

The Pigs and the Pinder

Pinfold Street acquires its name from the 'pinfold', or pound, that existed on the south side of the lane as early as 1592. The latest one survived until 1835, when it was demolished to make way for street widening. The 'Pinder' was the man in charge of the pinfold, a person extremely disliked and regarded as the common foe.

In the old days the community combined to hire a swineherd to look after their pigs. He would take the pigs to common land outside the little town. When the swineherd sounded his horn, pigs would rush from every direction, from houses, shops, grinding wheels and 'swyne howles' (pigsties). They would rush down entries and gennels with joyous grunts.

Later it became the habit to allow the pigs to roam the streets, grubbing amongst the refuse which was very abundant.

Near Christmas, many a working man's family were put on short rations, the food saved being used to fatten the pigs. Troughs were situated at the doors of most of the houses in the town and the pigs would feed on the public footpath. The pigs were summoned by their owners rattling the pig trough and it was amazing how they would rush to heed the call.

This annoyed the Pinder exceedingly, for when he was trying to run a wandering pig into the pinfold, and so claim four pence for its return, the owner would set up a great clattering and the pig would escape, to be safely housed before the Pinder could catch up with it!

The Stupid Club

The Stupid Club was a Sick and Dividing Club, more sick than dividing! It met in the old Blue Bell Inn[23] in Worksop Road, Attercliffe, in the 1880s. The members would meet to argue on any topic and the meetings usually ended in fighting.

The funds of the club were divided mainly in the form of liquid refreshment, the sick money never being drawn because of a rule that said a member had to give a fortnight's notice before being ill!

The Chairman was called the Spill Major, he sat nearest the fire and when a member required a light for his pipe, the Major lit a paper spill and passed it to him.

The Spill Major was also supposed to keep the members in order, but when he tried they would not listen. They were too stupid!

Johannaites. (Johanna's Secret Box of Writings)

In 1824 there existed a chapel in Coal Pit Lane (now Cambridge Street) that had belonged to the religious sect called Johannaites. These people were followers of a lady called Johanna Southcott who, it was expected, would give birth to a new Messiah.

One devoted follower who lived on the east side of Nursery Street, near the Wicker end, had a beautiful cradle made to hold the baby Messiah. Unfortunately, on December 27th, 1814, Johanna died, at the age of 60, still undelivered!

NOTES

1. This was, and still is, the area at the end of London Road near the Moor Foot. Some of the old cottages still exist, now converted into shops.
2. In olden times it was the custom to throw rice over the bride and bridegroom as a symbol of fertility. Today paper confetti is used for the same purpose.
3. The bronze statue by Burnard was erected in the Market Place in 1854, six years after Elliott's death. It was removed to Weston Park in 1875 when the roadway was widened.
4. The Court Leet or Court of 'Sembly Quest was the people's own court guaranteed to them by Lord Furnival. Minor offences, such as defiling the town wells or failure to scour ditches, were dealt with, the judges and jury being the people themselves.
5. There appears to be no substance to this story as Hunter, the historian, tells of a 'pile of stones called Ringinglawe' being mentioned in 1559. Nor is there any record existing of any bequest to the bell ringers of the Parish Church at this time.
6. In the year 1783, Frank Fern robbed and murdered a Sheffield jeweller who was passing over Loxley Common. Fern was captured the following day and after his trial he was executed, his body being hung in chains on a gibbet near the scene of his crime.
7. This was a very ancient coaching inn, first mentioned in the Burgery Accounts of 1572.
8. This stood at the corner of Button Lane and Backfields and was demolished to make way for Charter Square and the Grosvenor Hotel block of buildings. This inn should not be confused with the more famous hostelry of the same name that existed in Angel Street.
9. This is now channelled under the Moorfoot. The saw-mill stood approximately at the junction of Ecclesall Road and The Moor.
10. This cottage was situated in the centre of what is now St Mary's Gate and where the Brunswick Chapel of 1834 formerly stood. Little Sheffield was a collection of cottages stretching from the Porter to Hill Street.
11. This was the name given to what is now London Road, between Little Sheffield and Highfield.
12. This building can still be seen situated between Sharrow Lane and Sitwell Road. It is now a Community Centre.

13. Heeley Mill and water-wheel were situated near the footbridge from Saxon Road which crosses the Sheaf to Broadfield Road. Heeley Mill existed before the year 1600.

14. This stood near Broadfield Road, at the end of the footpath from Little London Road. At Smithy Wood three water-wheels were in use, one for tripping the hammer, one for driving the blowers and one for operating the grinding wheel. These water-wheels were in existence in 1496. One wheel still remained, in a ruined state, in the 1930s. The large dam is now filled in and works have been built on the site. Smithy Wood extended from the dam up the hillside to Scarsdale Top.

15. This little well, like the dam and wheels, has completely disappeared.

16. The tilt hammer known as Norton Hammer is no more, but a few old cottages remain to remind us of the water-wheels and works that existed there as long ago as 1560. The future of these cottages is uncertain.

17. A narrow lane, The Dale, is still in existence, but the Dale Farm, where Gillot, of steel pen nib fame, was born, was demolished in 1965. The joists and beams of the old farmhouse were solid rough-hewn oak tree trunks and the walls were of stone two feet thick. A modern factory now stands on this site.

18. This would be somewhere near the site of the present Big Tree Hotel.

19. This was situated down a small lane opposite the bottom of Cobnar Road.

20. Now the very pleasant Abbey Lane.

21. A considerable amount of beauty still remains in this area. Luckily this vicinity includes Millhouses Park, Beauchief Gardens and the extensive Ecclesall Woods.

22. This was originally a spring of water in the centre of a pleasant grove of trees. After the houses were built in this area, a stone with the inscription 'Spring Garden Well' could be seen in the garden of a house at the corner of Gell Street and Conway Street. This has long since disappeared.

23. The building is still in existence, but the old public house has now become a warehouse.

INDEX